THE LITTLE BOOK OF TOURISTS IN ICELAND

To Julia

Enjoy the trip!

Don't forget, the shark pickles are the best! just like my feet

Love

ALDA SIGMUNDSDÓTTIR

THE LITTLE BOOK OF TOURISTS IN ICELAND

TIPS, TRICKS,
AND WHAT THE ICELANDERS
REALLY THINK OF YOU

LITTLE BOOKS
PUBLISHING

TABLE OF CONTENTS

Introduction

Halló, og velkomin til Íslands!

That means "hello, and welcome to Iceland", in case you hadn't guessed.

For centuries, we Icelanders have enjoyed welcoming guests to our beautiful country, of which we are duly proud. What's not to love? The landscapes are stunning, the geology is amazing, the history is fascinating, it is clean, it is safe (provided you use your common sense), and it is one of the few places in the world where you can totally get away from the hordes.

Or at least that *was* the case, until a few years ago. Now it seems the whole world has discovered Iceland, a place that used to be frequented primarily by eccentrics who didn't mind navigating the rough terrain and rudimentary infrastructure outside the capital. Seemingly overnight, visitor numbers have exploded. Little old Iceland now draws hundreds of thousands of tourists a year from all over the world—each with their own set of hopes and expectations.

At the time of writing this, the population of Iceland is around 380,000 people. In 2010, when the tourist boom started in earnest, just short of half a million visitors came to the country.

At the height of the tourism boom prior to the outbreak of the Covid pandemic (the years 2017-2019), the number of foreign guests exceeded two million per year, approximately six times the population of Iceland. As this is written in 2023 tourism is once again in full swing, after a predictable lull during Covid.

Needless to say, this gives rise to a plethora of issues and challenges. The Icelandic people struggle to come to grips with this massive influx over so short a period and the resulting changes to their lives. Meanwhile our esteemed visitors are often largely unaware of the wide-reaching impact that their presence is having—both positive and negative. Many of them care deeply about Iceland, have made repeated trips to the country, and are very concerned about the effect that tourism is having on a place so close to their hearts. They want to know how to interact with locals in a way that is respectful and unobtrusive. They are curious about what Icelandic authorities are doing to protect Iceland's environment and culture. They are indignant on Iceland's behalf when they hear stories of the reckless and irresponsible behaviour of other tourists, and they want to help facilitate conscientious tourism. And they are curious about how the Icelanders feel about this invasion into their day-to-day lives.

The topic of tourism is expansive and very complex. It touches all facets of daily life. There is not a single Icelander that is not affected by it, yet everyone is affected in their own way, depending on their own personal circumstances. I harbour no illusions of being able to illuminate every corner of the subject in this book. What I can do is to try and touch upon some of the major issues, address the questions that I most often receive from people outside of Iceland, and give examples that may provide some insight into the various problems and challenges that the Icelanders are facing.

A caveat: writing about the subject of tourism in Iceland anno 2023 is a tricky business. New questions and challenges arise constantly, and responses to them are still very much in flux. Regulations are being amended, measures being implemented, government policies constantly changing, and so on. I ask for your understanding that some of the details in this book may be out of date by the time you read it. I have tried my best to omit facts and data that are very changeable and to focus on the broad strokes, yet there will be cases where figures and facts will have changed by the time you, the reader, hold this book in your hand. Where I do cite figures, I have done my best to find the most recent ones possible.

In writing this book, I have drawn on questions, observations and gripes from both Icelanders and non-Icelanders. As an author of several books about Iceland who has been fairly active on social media for a number of years, I am in the privileged position of being in perpetual dialogue with the group for which my books are primarily written—the Icelandophiles, expats, and others who care about Iceland and are interested in Icelandic affairs. As an Icelander, I also enjoy the advantage of going behind the language barrier and observing the discussions and debates that take place in Icelandic—a barrier, I might add, that is very high for most outsiders, given the obscurity and complication of the Icelandic language.

All that being said, I am not an expert in the tourism field. I am a layperson, a casual observer, discussing this expansive, overarching subject as it appears "from the doorway of my farmhouse", to borrow an old Icelandic idiom. Also, I apologize in advance if it seems I am being judgmental or negative about tourists ... it is certainly not my intention. Yet sometimes the truth needs to be spoken, and some people may take personal offense where none is intended. At times I get irritated when tourists do stupid things that infringe upon other people's lives or cause them discomfort. At the same time I can get massively annoyed at Icelanders when *they* do stupid things, like waffle and vacillate on important issues such as protecting Icelandic nature or improving safety for our visitors.

Finally: this is not a guidebook. It will not inform you about the best restaurants, the most inexpensive tours, where to observe the northern lights, or suchlike. There is an abundance of books, websites and forums to help you with those sorts of questions. I hope instead to help facilitate some understanding of the massive changes that tourism is having on the social fabric of Iceland.

ICELAND AND THE TOURISM BOOM

The good, the bad and the ...

If you were to ask an Icelander about the positive and negative aspects of the tourism boom, most would probably say something along these lines:

Good

✓ Tourism rescued our economy when it needed rescuing the most. We are super happy to have all these people coming in and spending their money here.

✓ My parents are renting out their basement to tourists. My sister started a business servicing Airbnb units for landlords. My best friend is conducting walking tours downtown. People are finally making some money around here.

✓ Iceland needs foreign currency coming in so we can buy stuff from abroad. We also need to have a reserve for the lean years. The tourism boom has given us both.

✓ After the economic crash, downtown Reykjavík was like a ghost town. Empty storefronts, no people. These days it is filled with tourists and new restaurants and cafés seem to be opening every day. Lots more choice for us locals, too. It's great!

✓ Remember the days when Icelandair was basically the only way to get off the rock because there were no other airlines? You couldn't go abroad without breaking the bank because of their damn monopoly. We Icelanders subsidized their cheap flight tickets for foreign passengers because we didn't have a choice. Now? So many airlines flying to Iceland, so much competition. Finally we can have reasonable airline tickets like everyone else!

Bad

✗ All our natural sites are overcrowded now. I went to Jökulsárlón last week and there were around 100 cars in the parking lot. Only a few years ago I would go there and there would be, like, five cars besides ours. It's too crowded. I want my country back.

✗ The path up to my favourite waterfall is now a muddy mess, and people have started going outside of it so pretty soon that will be trampled, too. And the moss around the riverbank is almost all gone. Our nature is being destroyed by foot traffic, and I can't see how the smaller municipalities will be able to fund the construction of boardwalks or make improvements to protect natural sites in their area.

✗ I never go into downtown Reykjavík anymore because everything is so overpriced. All the tourist areas are so expensive. And can we talk about the Blue Lagoon!? They've jacked up their prices by something like 80 percent in the past few years. Taking a five-person family to the Blue Lagoon costs about the same as flying abroad for two people. It's insane.

✗ I belong to a hiking group and every year we would do a four-day trip somewhere in Iceland. We would stay in sleeping-bag accommodation, which was easily affordable. Now, there is no way for us to do that anymore—not only have prices soared, everything is totally booked in the summer. As a result we have had to give up our wonderful annual hikes in Iceland, and we are discussing going abroad, some place where our budget allows. We can't afford to travel in our own country anymore.

✗ I went downtown last weekend and of the three places we went, none of the service staff spoke Icelandic. I can't even go out in my country these days and speak my own language.

✗ I just came back from a hike and there was toilet paper everywhere along the trail. At one point I veered off to the side and just barely avoided stepping into a big pile of shit that someone had left there. I know there are no toilets around, and the local authorities should probably put up some port-a-potties near the parking lot, but this trail used to only have a few people on it, up to a couple of years ago. In all the years I have been hiking there I have never seen toilet paper anywhere, and now I see it all over. It's gross.

✗ What really bothers me is how some Icelanders are screwing people over and taking advantage of them. They take tourists up on the glaciers, which is so dangerous, without even a proper license. And what about all the people who ask for "volunteers" from abroad to come work in Iceland in return for, say, getting to go on free horse riding tours or whatever, but basically treat them as slaves and pay them nothing. It's disgusting, and makes me ashamed to be Icelandic.

I should tell you that these are not direct quotes. I adapted them based on the things I hear constantly from Icelanders all around me. As you can see, opinions differ, but one thing everyone can agree on is that the tourism issue is complex and, right now at least, a tad overwhelming.

So how did it come to this?

In late 2008, the Icelandic nation was plunged into a nightmare of epic proportions. Its three commercial banks collapsed in quick succession, the Icelandic króna plummeted in value, and the country teetered on the edge of national bankruptcy. People lost their jobs, their homes, their livelihoods; inflation and private debt soared, and the national deficit became a big, black hole. Imported goods (which in Iceland means practically everything) doubled or tripled in price, virtually overnight. Worse, there was not enough foreign currency to buy basics like food, gasoline or prescription drugs from abroad. Things started running out in the stores. It was terrifying.

Icelandic authorities had no choice but to seek help. The International Monetary Fund came to the rescue with a big loan, and slowly the economy began to recover. Various factors helped, one of them being the favourable exchange rate. Since the króna had suddenly lost around half its value, travel to this previously costly destination had become affordable, and people who in the past had thought of visiting suddenly saw a good opportunity to go.

Then, just as tourism was starting to work its magic, a volcano nestled deep inside the Eyjafjallajökull glacier stirred, rumbled and blew its top, disgorging a massive cloud of ash into the atmosphere. Air traffic was grounded for days, passengers became stranded, and general mayhem prevailed. If Iceland's financial crisis had not put the country firmly on the map, the unruly volcano with the unpronounceable name most definitely did. The eyes of the world collectively turned, and saw Iceland.

Tourism authorities panicked. No one would want to visit the country now. Not only was it a financial mess, it was obviously far too dangerous. The eruption, they concluded despondently, would snuff out a fledgling industry that had held so much promise for the economic recovery of the nation.

But Icelanders have never been known to surrender without a fight. With (literally) a huge dark cloud looming, tourism authorities went on the offensive. They hired a savvy British PR firm to create a video that featured people bopping around in amazing scenery and getting naked out in nature, all set to the jaunty sounds of Emiliana Torrini's Jungle Drum. The battle plan: get every single Icelander to share the hell out of that video on social media, and to get their friends to do the same. Make it go viral. Make Iceland great again.

It worked. Before the ash had settled from Eyjafjallajökull's final belch, the "Inspired by Iceland" campaign had taken off like a racehorse with a firecracker up its butt. In 2010, the year Eyjafjallajökull erupted, there were some 490,000 visitors to Iceland. In 2019, the last year prior to the Covid pandemic that might be considered "normal" in terms of travel, just short of two million visitors came to Iceland. In summer 2022 the tourism industry in Iceland was once again robust—the number of nights in tourist accommodation in July 2022 was the highest ever recorded, or more than 1.5 million.

So yes, the promotional campaign delivered. That's the upside. The downside: Icelandic authorities, eager as they were to stoke the fire, were completely unprepared for the inferno they set off. Iceland's infrastructure was in no way equipped to handle all those visitors. Tourism brought much-needed cash to Iceland, but also greed, exploitation and slipping standards. Icelandic authorities have struggled to come to grips with the problem, but the solutions have not been straightforward. While the omissions are not as glaring as they were in the early days of mass tourism, and while much good has been done to protect natural sites and ensure the safety of visitors, there are still many areas of this huge, expansive issue that require work. After all, there are many interests at stake, and many powerful individuals who stand to profit from certain policies, or lack thereof.

On that note, let us zoom in.

Sleep 'n stay

Over this past decade or so, one of the most urgent questions facing Iceland has been where all those people were supposed to sleep. Indeed, finding accommodation in Iceland during the high season has been like throwing dice in a craps game. You may win, but you'll most probably lose. That is, unless you have booked months or even years in advance.

So what to do?

The default solution of local authorities has been to build more hotels. Indeed, in 2019 and 2020, some 1,500 rooms in newly constructed hotels became available throughout Iceland.

Which is all good and fine, though also worrying because: Who wants to live in an area where there are only hotels? (No one, that's who.) What is going to happen when tourists only meet other tourists, and the local flavour of the area is gone—as is already happening with certain areas in downtown Reykjavík?

More on that in a separate section.

As for the initial conundrum, the solution that presented itself and pretty much saved the day was one that has come to the rescue in many other tourist destinations: Airbnb. The home-sharing, home-renting platform that is loved and reviled in equal measure. Airbnb stepped in to fill the gap, and has by now firmly established itself on the Icelandic market, from which it is unlikely to retreat any time soon, especially given the fact that Airbnb rentals are usually far less expensive than hotel accommodation. In a country like Iceland where prices tend to be on the steep side (to put it mildly), finding bargains is essential for many people.

A recent study by the Central Bank of Iceland estimated that 10 percent of all properties in the country were listed on Airbnb in 2017. After a brief reversal during the Covid pandemic, when rentals suddenly became plentiful due to the absence of tourists, we now see the same trend—so much that in May 2022 the Icelandic Tenants' Association declared a "state of emergency" on the housing market, due to the absence of available long-term rental housing.

Even before the influx of tourism, Iceland's rental market was *tiny*. The reason is that most people own their own homes, and aren't in the business of renting them unless they go away somewhere for a good while. Such people, who might at one time have looked for a family or student to occupy their rental property, now know that they can make far more money renting out short-term to tourists than long-term to regular tenants. A fact that has shrunk an already-minuscule rental market down to virtually nothing.

This obviously poses difficulty for locals who need a roof over their heads and who are not in a position to buy. Very often these are young people who may or may not be starting a family, and whose savings are nil. The types of properties that are particularly suitable for them are the ones that are centrally located (so you don't need a car) and are not too large—exactly the types of apartments that can fetch the highest prices on Airbnb.

Jumping through hoops

Back to Airbnb. The way it is impacting the rental market is not exclusive to Iceland. All over the world local authorities are trying to figure out the best way to curb Airbnb rentals in an effort to maintain balance on their housing markets.

Icelandic authorities are no exception, and have been test-driving various measures. Until the beginning of 2017 it was illegal to rent out property through Airbnb without a special permit. Obtaining said permit meant running a gauntlet of red tape that rivalled East German administration circa 1980. Anyone who wanted to legally list their property on Airbnb, even if it was just a room in their house, had to obtain the same licence as someone who wanted to open a hotel or guesthouse. This meant obtaining about twenty different signatures from various bureaucrats around the country, plus diverse inspections and certifications, all with the requisite wait times and such. The sheer enormity of the task tended to put people off, and many decided they'd rather risk being busted than go through the gruelling process of obtaining a licence. And so, hundreds upon hundreds of Airbnb properties in Reykjavík came to be listed without a permit. This infuriated hotel and guesthouse operators, who had gone through the whole endorsement trial with all the associated costs, and they put pressure on government and law enforcement to get those bandits off the market, stat. And this is how it came to be that some poor hapless tourists went to open the doors of their rental Airbnb unit in their underwear, only to find officers in full uniform standing outside, sternly asking to see the licence for their flat. (For the record, no tourist was ever evicted by police, but their Airbnb landlords would have received a visit, and a sizeable fine.)

This system was not effective for anyone, something needed to change, and the most obvious solution was to draft new laws. These laws took effect at the beginning of 2017 and allow homeowners to rent out all or part of their home for up to 90 days a year, or until their earnings reach ISK 2 million (USD 14,000), without applying for the dreaded licence. The only thing they need to do is to register their property with the local police department, and pay a nominal fee. This, it is hoped, will combat tax evasion and give authorities a more comprehensive picture of the Airbnb market. It will also derail speculators, those professional Airbnb hosts who, flush with tourist dollars, snap up all available flats in coveted areas in order to turn them into tourist apartments, outbidding any normal person who is not a direct participant in the tourism gold rush. Moreover, it allows regular folks to rent out their apartments for a part of the year, allowing them to finance that dream vacation, the home renovation that has been on the agenda for years, or even just their mortgage payments.

Win-win.

The draw of flight

The boom in tourism, then, has made things difficult for Icelanders on the rental market. So is tourism making it impossible for Icelanders to live in their own country? Or "has tourism brought new job opportunities for Icelanders, or has it created mostly low-paying service jobs that the Icelanders don't really want to fill," as a reader of my newsletter wanted to know?

Tourism has certainly created new opportunities for Icelanders, and led to various forms of entrepreneurship. Figures from Statistics Iceland reveal that from 2013-2017 the number of new businesses in the tourism industry grew by 42 percent, while new businesses *not* in the tourism industry increased by only 11 percent. At the end of 2016 there were 1,347 licensed travel agencies or tour operators in Iceland, of which 978 had received accreditation since 2010. This number had dropped to 478 in 2022, likely due to the effects of the Covid pandemic and factors like the bankruptcy of low-cost carrier WOW Air in 2019—yet in spite of this, the tourism industry accounted for 40 percent of Iceland's foreign currency revenues in 2022, making it the country's largest industry by far. Some people are prospering, and have happily found their place in the new world order (yours truly included). On the other hand, many of the new jobs created are indeed ones that Icelanders don't care to fill. Not because they think they are above that sort of work, but because they are overqualified. They are highly educated, with graduate or postgraduate degrees, and there are simply no opportunities in their respective fields.

It is incontestable, however, that the travel industry drains manpower from other fields, perhaps most notably (in Iceland, at least) the educational and medical systems. In both of those, people have grown disgruntled with a chronic lack of proper funding, which has resulted in added pressure on folks working in those fields. The problem is not new, but was taken to a new level during the Covid pandemic, when healthcare workers were subject to almost inhuman pressure at work. So, with tourism back on track, many workers have decided to move to jobs in the travel industry. Indeed, even prior to the Covid pandemic there was a visible trend of teaching and nursing professionals seeking careers as flight attendants—a job that allows for travel, which by extension allows for shopping overseas, which is tantamount to a pay rise since it gives people so much more spending power with their hard-earned salaries. In contrast to teaching or nursing, airline jobs are fairly well paid, working conditions are good-to-excellent, you don't take your work home with you, and there is usually plenty of free time between flights. It is easy to see the draw.

Call the law, or not

Another sector that has been hard hit by the tourism boom is law enforcement. As with medical professionals and teachers, Icelandic police officers complain of an excessive workload and there is an exodus from the profession. In 2007 there were 2.3 police officers per 1,000 inhabitants in Iceland. In 2022, that number was 1.9 officers per 1,000 inhabitants. At the same time, the number of tourists to our island has more than quadrupled on an annual basis (Covid years excluded), and violent crimes have become much more frequent.

I am often asked why the Icelanders are not more diligent when it comes to fining or arresting people who damage Iceland's sensitive environment or violate the law in some way. Short answer: absence of manpower. Iceland is a large and sparsely populated island, and there simply are not enough police officers to go around.

Klondike

It seems strange, what with all those people coming in and the revenues they leave behind, that basic institutions in Iceland like schools, hospitals and even law enforcement should be so underfunded. Surely those two million people per year can help fund health care and education for a mere 380,000 souls. Right? Which begs the question: where does the money go?

Alas, that is not easily answered without launching into a lengthy treatise about the structure of the Icelandic economy and political sector. Suffice it to say that the distribution of wealth leaves a lot to be desired in Iceland, just as it does in many other places. Those who have connections to the "right" political party tend to have the rules bent, or laws outright changed, to serve their own interest at the expense of the little folk.

Case in point: there is a company in Iceland called Reykjavík Excursions (RE) that operates a shuttle bus to and from Keflavík Airport, plus various tours out of Reykjavík. Initially owned by Icelandair, it is now owned by parties closely affiliated with the aforementioned "right" party (the father, mother and uncle of current minister of finance and economic affairs, and former prime minister, Bjarni Benediktsson of the Independence Party, to be precise). For years Reykjavík Excursions had a monopoly on the route connecting Keflavík Airport with

Reykjavík, meaning no other coach company was allowed to drive that route. The monopoly was a source of much contention among bus companies in Iceland, since the Reykjavík-KEF route is highly lucrative, as you can likely imagine. The monopoly was finally overturned, but as RE was the only company driving on that route for so many years, it has managed to keep its strong position on the market. Moreover, RE has enjoyed evident favour with the Icelandic government, as when the aforesaid Bjarni Benediktsson granted tax exemptions to coach companies that appeared to be tailor-made for his family members and their business interests.

Indeed, tourism is to Iceland today approximately what banking was in the 2000s. It is the new Klondike industry, the place to which profiteers gravitate. It is, therefore, not surprising that one of Iceland's disgraced bankers, who in 2013 received a sentence of five and a half years for market manipulation, has got into the tourism business. From inside his white-collar prison he managed to reinvent himself as a hotel mogul, and now owns, in full or part, seven hotels in Iceland, including the ION Luxury Adventure Hotel near Nesjavellir in South Iceland and Hótel Búðir on Snæfellsnes.

Another disconcerting trend that has been emerging is that operations that have been built up by individuals and smaller enterprises are being forcibly taken over by larger concerns when they start turning a significant profit. One example is an unnamed exhibition that was developed and built up over the course of four years by a husband-and-wife team. During their first year, they received some 20,000 guests, and lost money. By year three, after substantial investment and tireless promotion, the number had risen to 94,000 guests. In year four, the company that owns the premises that houses the exhibition decided not to renew the lease, and to take over the exhibition and related gift shop themselves.

I could list several more such examples, but I'm sure I don't need to. You get the picture. The big fish push aside the little fry to get to the tasty morsels, as soon as the morsels start getting tasty. Never mind that it was the little fry that made the morsels in the first place—such details are insubstantial.

Blue gold

Then there is the story of the Blue Lagoon.

Once upon a time, this site that is today *the* most iconic tourist attraction in Iceland, was no more than a small pond out in the middle of a lava field. The year was 1976, and it had accidentally formed through the run-off from a nearby geothermal power plant. One day a local resident with psoriasis discovered that this pastel-hued puddle, coloured baby blue by the proliferation of silica in its water, seemed to have a positive effect on his skin condition. Soon word got around that the pool near the

Svartsengi (Black Field) power plant contained healing properties. In those days the lagoon was completely undeveloped and the lava rock at the bottom was so sharp that you were lucky to get through a whole bathing session without slicing your foot open. Still, folks put up with it because the experience of sitting in a deliciously warm pool of silica-rich water next to a steam-belching power plant was kind of amazing.

There were no proper facilities at the lagoon back then, and the bohemians who went there had to make do with the back seat of their car or hollows in the lava to get changed for their soak. Before long, however, the place started to gain in popularity, and a makeshift change room, vaguely resembling a shipping container, was deposited on the banks of the lagoon so folks could at least take a shower after their dip.

At this time, the Blue Lagoon, as it was dubbed, was still owned by the Svartsengi power plant. With the lagoon's popularity growing, the operators of the plant put out a request for tenders for companies to construct proper facilities. The contract went to two business partners from Keflavík. They set about building proper change and shower rooms, and had big plans for the site, including moving the lagoon to another location and constructing much larger facilities that included a health centre.

In 1987, the first year in which the pair assumed operations of the Blue Lagoon, some 35,000 guests visited the site. By 1990, thanks to their diligent promotion and development, the number had risen to 80,000 and the site's popularity kept growing. It was then that the township of Grindavík, situated a few kilometres to the south of the site, formally requested authority to assume operations of the Blue Lagoon, on the grounds that this would better ensure the safety of the bathers that were now visiting the site. Which, loosely translated, probably meant: "Now that the Blue Lagoon is churning gold we would kindly like to take it over."

What followed was a nasty bout of political wrangling, conflict and bad blood. The power plant, the formal owner of the Blue Lagoon, was jointly owned by five separate townships in the area. The township of Grindavík, however, had sole planning authority over the site on which the lagoon was located, and could therefore make or break plans for the location of a new Blue Lagoon. Which, ultimately, it did, changing zoning laws so that the site that the two partners had had in mind for the new lagoon was made into an industrial area. Today, however, the new Blue Lagoon happens to be located very near that original site.

I will spare you the nitty-gritty details, but suffice it to say that, through some murky dealings and other shenanigans, the Blue Lagoon has managed to make a handful of people very rich. Today it is a huge player on the Icelandic tourism scene. Not only is it the most popular tourist destination in the country, it also collects the highest admission charge of any other site. It is owned by a consortium of shareholders, the largest single owner being a man named Grímur Sæmundsson, who is also its CEO. In 2019 alone, the Blue Lagoon returned a profit of ISK 3 billion, just short of USD 21 million.

The Blue Lagoon has come a long way from its humble origins as a small pond in the midst of the lava. When the first facilities were put up, the price of admission was ISK 100, the same as admission to a local pool. Today a visit to the Blue Lagoon will set you back from ISK 8,990 per person (USD 59 and up … there are no listed prices for the exclusive Retreat Spa package, only that a visit starts at USD 411 for up to four hours), depending on the time of day you visit and the level of luxury you want. And it is not like those steep prices have reduced its popularity—since the summer of 2016 you have to book your visit in advance if you want guaranteed admission.

In contrast to its early days, however, the popularity of the lagoon today is almost exclusively among foreign visitors, who make up 98 percent of its customers. Icelanders, who once flocked there, have largely stopped going, put off by the masses of tourists and the ever-rising prices. A few years ago, it was a place to go when you wanted to treat yourself, to share a romantic outing, or to take visitors from abroad. Not so anymore.

In early 2020, at the beginning of the Covid pandemic, the Blue Lagoon was the subject of public outrage when it became one of the first companies to make use of measures introduced by the Icelandic government to help stave off bankruptcies and protect jobs. Under this scheme, companies could apply to have the government pay 75 percent of staff wages—in other words, companies on the Icelandic market were being given unprecedented access to taxpayer's money, to help them survive an unprecedented crisis. One of the first companies in line was the Blue Lagoon—one of the biggest and wealthiest companies in Iceland, that moreover had paid out over ISK 7.8 billion (51 million USD) in dividends to its handful of shareholders over the three years preceding the pandemic. Predictably, this resulted in widespread fury: surely the Blue Lagoon had sufficient resources to cover unexpected setbacks without having to resort to public funding to keep it afloat?

The operators of the Blue Lagoon Ltd. have certainly succeeded in turning what is effectively wastewater dumped into a natural landscape into a wildly popular tourist attraction. As such, they deserve credit, even if a few toes were allegedly stepped on to get there. Don't they?

The scramble for ownership

Which brings me to another hot-potato topic: the race to snap up sites that can be exploited for profit.

The wealth mongers, always on the lookout for good investments, now circle Iceland's various attractions hawk-like, waiting for the chance to swoop down and snap them up. Like for instance one of Iceland's most beautiful and iconic locations, the Jökulsárlón glacier lagoon.

The land surrounding the lagoon has for decades been owned by a consortium of private individuals, and there have been running disputes over its future development. In the end the owners decided to sell the land, and in November 2016 Jökulsárlón and its surrounding regions were acquired by an investment fund for ISK 1.5 billion (USD 10 million). The acquisition came after the Icelandic state waived its pre-emptive rights to buy the site, on the grounds that it did not have the funds. Now, you may be thinking that this news prompted some debate in Icelandic society, with concerned citizens pushing for Jökulsárlón's protection and others arguing for the state to keep its hands off. Not so. The news of the acquisition came and went, and barely a discussion arose. The Icelandic people on the whole seemed neither interested nor concerned that one of their most stunning natural wonders was being sold off to ambiguous owners, fronted by an investment fund.

The Icelandic state had three months to reverse its decision to buy the site and annul the acquisition. Finally, with just two days to spare, the then-outgoing prime minister of Iceland ruled that the state would indeed claim its pre-emptive rights and purchase the site. But lo! The heads of the investment fund pointed out that it was too late—the period of grace afforded to the state to reverse the decision had to be calculated from the time when the investment fund's offer was accepted, and not when the District Magistrate's Office approved the acquisition, two days later. A flurry of panic ensued while attorneys fought over whether or not the state had let this natural gem slip through its fingers. A few days later a ruling was passed that all had been by the book, and that Jökulsárlón now belonged to the Icelandic people. In July 2017, Jökulsárlón was formally declared a protected site by the Icelandic government, and incorporated into Vatnajökull National Park. This story, at least, ended happily.

Yet this is not the only site of exceptional natural beauty that is coveted by investors. In 2022, the Fjaðrárgljúfur canyon, made famous by Justin Bieber when he used it in a 2015 music video, was sold to a private company for ISK 280 million (just under 2 million USD). The sale came after the Icelandic state waived its pre-emptive rights to purchase the site, though it does retain that right if the site is put up for sale again. In the years prior to the sale, the Icelandic state paid out some ISK 50 million for viewing platforms, paths, and toilet facilities on the site. The new owners have pledged to "work towards having the canyon declared a protected site" and to still allow access for tourists, yet they will be introducing a parking fee—something that previously was free.

Other natural sites that have recently been bought by (foreign) investors are the historical promontory Hjörleifshöfði, in south Iceland, and large stretches of land in East Iceland with salmon fishing rivers running through them.

TOURING ICELAND, STAYING SAFE
60

Come prepared

In 2009, there were seven airlines with regular scheduled flights to Iceland. In summer 2022 that number had risen to 24 airlines. Quite a jump, I am sure you will agree.

At the risk of sounding elitist, one of the changes Icelanders have noticed over that period is that the type of people who visit has, well, broadened. Prior to the tourist boom, people who chose to visit Iceland tended to be reasonably well informed about the country. They had done a bunch of research, and generally came prepared. They knew, for instance, that they should never go up on a glacier without a guide, and that they should not hike up a mountain wearing a pair of sneakers on their feet.

But as Iceland became increasingly trendy and flights proliferated, more and more people started to arrive without any real understanding of its nature or climate. Perhaps they had seen a bunch of pictures on Instagram or Facebook, then saw an enticing offer online, and made an impulsive decision to book a flight, without knowing what sorts of conditions would greet them.

We see this in people arriving in completely unsuitable clothing, heading out into situations that they have entirely underestimated, and generally putting themselves at risk in ways that we were not used to with our guests in the past.

Preamble over: let us look at some of the essential things to keep in mind when you visit Iceland.

Before we go further

A public service announcement:

This would probably be a good time to inform you about safetravel.is. This website par excellence is run by the Icelandic Search and Rescue Association (ICE-SAR) and any visitor to Iceland should give it a thorough perusal before embarking on their trip, and check it often while in the country. Among other things it lists any alerts or warnings pertaining to weather, road closures, volcanic eruptions or whatever else a traveller needs to know. It also offers a multitude of tips for making your journey a safe one, and best of all, allows you to leave a travel itinerary online so that if you don't arrive on time at your intended destination they'll know something may be wrong. They will even monitor your trip, if you so wish. Through the website you can also rent a Personal Location Beacon (PLB) that can be used in emergencies to summon assistance and which is far more reliable than a mobile phone, since it works even where there is no mobile service.

Mind you these are not the only websites that travellers to Iceland should bookmark—a more comprehensive list is included at the end of this book.

/public service announcement

Safety

Staying safe has become a major concern in a world that seems more and more treacherous by the day. In fact, one of the proposed reasons for Iceland's booming popularity is that, in a world where terrorist attacks and other scary happenings seem to be on the rise, it has remained safe.

But is it really?

Examined in the above context, yes it is. There has never been a terrorist attack in Iceland (touch wood) and the crime rate is relatively low. However, that does not mean that nothing bad ever happens, that people never get attacked, taken advantage of, or robbed. (I wish.)

Iceland has crime like every other place. There are thefts, drug-related crimes, sexual assaults, muggings. People get roofied (date rape drugs put in their drinks, in case you're not up on your sexual-assault slang), murdered, stabbed … all that ugly stuff.

In almost all violent crime cases, there is some sort of relationship between victim and perpetrator. Random assaults are rare, though they do happen, and then usually when there are inebriants involved. What we had not seen in Iceland before January 2017 was the sort of crime where a person is abducted by someone they do not know, assaulted, and then murdered. Then it happened.

The murder of Birna Brjánsdóttir, a twenty-year old woman who had been out partying in downtown Reykjavík and either got in voluntarily or was forced into a car with her assailant, devastated the Icelandic nation. The case marked a certain loss of innocence for Iceland, which we all mourned to a greater or lesser degree.

By all of this I wish to say, do not assume that Iceland is crime-free. Exercise the same caution you would in other places: do not accept rides with strangers, stick to well-lit roads if you are walking at night, watch your drinks in bars, watch your belongings (especially in bars), and keep your wits about you.

The hazards of nature

But safety, of course, is not exclusively about crime. Our foreign visitors are statistically far more likely to come to harm through accidents, either out in nature or on the roads, than through assaults or muggings in downtown Reykjavík. Looked at that way, Iceland is probably *less* safe than many other locations that you might visit.

Iceland's nature is awe-inspiring, and the landscape can be dangerous. We locals have learned pretty well to navigate the hazards, partly because a deep respect for our volatile nature has been instilled in us from childhood. This is not always so with our guests. Many of them hail from large cities, or urban areas that have different sorts of dangers than Iceland does. On hearing the words "storm" or "blizzard" or "surf" or "undertow", they may picture something quite different from what we Icelanders do. They may moreover be used to precautions being taken on their behalf, such as big fences or blazing billboards being erected where there are dangers. We Icelanders, on the other hand, have not been in the habit of installing those, mostly because until now we haven't much needed to.

"Until now" being the operative phrase. As visitor numbers increase, so do the number of fatal accidents, usually because our foreign visitors underestimate the hazards of our land. And we Icelanders can't quite work out what to do. Do we put up more signs? We could, but that would ruin one of Iceland's major draws: its raw, unspoiled vistas. Do we have guards patrol certain locations year-round, ensuring our guests don't put their lives at risk? Perhaps, but Iceland is vast, and putting security guards at every risky site around the country would be impossible.

In other words, please do not assume a site is safe just because there are no fences or signs there to alert you. Instead, use your common sense. Don't step too close to the edge of cliffs. Don't go too close to the surf to get a better picture. Those things. And in the rare locations where there *are* ropes or fences or signs, please respect them. The very fact that they are there will mean that there is a good reason.

Below are some common Icelandic hazards that you will

want to know about, though I should emphatically state that this list is not exhaustive.

Beaches with heavy surf

One of the most visited and photographed sites in Iceland is Reynisfjara beach, in the south. Its stunning scenery draws hundreds of visitors per day: a black stretch of sand, a cliff face with beautiful basalt columns, and iconic pillars rising out of the sea just offshore. Reynisfjara is a bit like our Times Square … when you finally visit it you feel like you've been there before because you've seen it in so many pictures.

Reynisfjara is a photographer's dream, and it is easy to become distracted there. Some people wade out into the surf to get a better picture, or turn their back to the water to snap photos of the basalt wall. But beware: that beach has some of the most dangerous undertows in the business. The waves that crash onto Reynisfjara can, and regularly do, pull the ground out from under people, causing them to lose their footing in the dissolving sand and immediately get pulled out by the churning waves. A number of people have drowned there. The fortunate ones have made a narrow escape, in some cases destroying expensive camera equipment in the process.

With five fatal accidents on or near Reynisfjara beach since 2015, Icelandic authorities are debating how best to respond

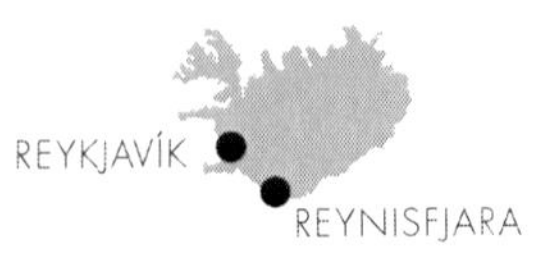

to the dangers in Reynisfjara and surrounding beaches. Touring companies that stop there regularly strongly emphasize the dangers to their clients, but also say that lots of people don't pay heed to their warnings. And in any case, not everyone travels to the beach with touring companies—many people do so on their own, in rental vehicles.

The thing about Reynisfjara, and other beaches that are exposed to the open sea, is that sometimes the waves don't seem that threatening. The day will be nice and calm, but there will be a strong undercurrent that people underestimate because the weather is so good. Also, some waves may roll lazily onto the shore, and then BAM you'll have a sneaker wave that crashes high onto the beach and can easily grab a person and carry them out to sea. This was the case in 2016 with a man who stood on a small rock with his back to the waves, taking pictures of his family. He was swept away without warning, and drowned.

Reynisfjara is one of those places that traditionally have not had big warning signs alerting people to the dangers. As an Icelander, you just knew that the waves on the beach could be extremely dangerous. After the accident in 2016, larger signs were put up in a more obvious location, and police patrolled the beach for several days.

Recently, there have been ever-more loud calls for a warden or guard to patrol Reynisfjara 24/7. Following serious accidents like those described above, the beaches are usually closed off for a while, or a police officer is stationed there for a time, at least while dangerous conditions persist. As yet, though, there are no definitive plans to have someone on call in Reynisfjara at all times.

Bottom line: Take care on Iceland's beaches. The surf can easily pull the ground out from under you, and the undertow can carry you away in the blink of an eye.

Hopping on the ice floes

As previously mentioned, an iconic and much-visited site is the Jökulsárlón glacier lagoon, a body of water created by the run-off from Vatnajökull glacier. Here large chunks of ice that have broken off the glacier float around for a while before being carried out to sea. A glacier lagoon, it goes without saying, is cold, and at some point in their lives Icelanders learn that falling into the water amongst the icebergs is something you most definitely want to avoid. Even if you were wearing a life vest you would probably only survive a few minutes in the frigid water, and without one you would likely seize up and drown before you even had a chance to turn blue.

Evidently some of our foreign guests were not sent this memo, or if they were, it has not quite been absorbed. I say

this because in the last few years there have been repeated photos and videos online of tourists heading out onto the ice floes, even hopping from one floating sheet of ice to another. Whole families have been caught on video engaging in this dangerous practice—even parents with their small children. People! Those are ice floes and icebergs! If floes become separated from the main ice mass you could easily float out to sea on your own little private island of ice, which probably sounds a whole lot more appealing than it actually is. As for icebergs, they have a habit of flipping over, and if you are on it when it flips … well you'd better say s'long because the suction it creates will take you down with it. And if you land under the ice, it will most likely be curtains for you.

Bottom line: Stay off the floating ice!

Glacier treks without an experienced guide

There is something truly extraordinary about being on or near a glacier. They have a powerful energy, an ancient, serene kind of forcefulness that cannot be adequately described in words. They also have a strange magnetism, and it can be very tempting to wander up onto one.

Don't do it. Even if it looks safe. The ice cover may appear uniform and thick, but a thin crust of ice may cover a crevice, up to a kilometre deep. Glaciers also have moulins, holes that are a product of ice melting and that extend deep into the ice cap, even down to the bottom of the glacier. I am sure I don't need to elaborate on the outcome if you fall into one of those.

There are other dangers, as well. For example, it is easy to lose your way on a glacier if you can no longer see your car or other signpost that helps you navigate. This can happen even if you do not go very far. A few years ago a Swedish photographer headed up onto Sólheimajökull glacier, likely with the intention of going only a short distance, as he was very poorly equipped. He lost his way, and managed to call for help, but was unable to say exactly where he was. He described the area, which seemed to correspond to a certain location, so rescue teams were dispatched there. After three days of searching the man's car was found in a completely different area. Soon afterwards he was found dead in a shallow crevice that, had he had spikes on his shoes, he could easily have climbed out of. Yet because he was wearing only regular street shoes, he kept slipping back down the sides of the crevice. A terrible tragedy that could easily have been prevented.

Bottom line: Never go anywhere on a glacier without an accredited, experienced tour guide who knows the area well.

Diving or snorkelling in Silfra

Silfra is a beautiful, fresh water ravine situated in Þingvellir National Park, where the Eurasian and North American tectonic plates meet. It attracts snorkelers and divers from all over the world who want to experience diving in the fissure between the two continental plates, in crystal-clear water that allows for a visibility of up to 80 metres. Silfra's popularity has grown in tandem with the tourist boom and in 2019 up to 300 people dove in Silfra daily.

But diving can be a risky sport, and from 2010 to March 2017 there were five fatal accidents in Silfra, and six near-fatal accidents. This earned the ravine the dubious honour of being the second-most dangerous place in Iceland—the first being the stretch of road between Reykjavík and Jökulsárlón glacier lagoon, in the south of the country. Two fatalities, a month apart, in Silfra in early 2017 generated much discussion about the number of people going into the ravine, and at times having to stand in line to enter the water in wet suits that may constrict the neck and potentially cause dizziness. In the wake of the 2017 fatality, Silfra was closed temporarily. When it reopened, safety requirements had been tightened considerably.

Bottom line: If you choose to snorkel or dive in Silfra, make sure that you are of sound health, that you comply with all safety regulations, and that you are aware of all and any risks.

Taking photographs

Obviously not dangerous per se, but rather how you might lose yourself in the act of taking that epic picture. It is easy to do. I have already mentioned the tragedy at Reynisfjara beach, where a man was taking a photograph of his family with his back to the surf. There have also been incidents when people have stood close to the edges of bird cliffs, absorbed in photographing the birds, and have fallen off the edge.

In Iceland there are literally photo opportunities at every turn. And far, far too many people stop their cars on the side of a road *or even in the middle of a highway* to photograph the scenery. I am not sure what possesses people to do so, unless it is that Icelandic highways are not of the major freeway-type variety that you get in some countries, so visitors may assume that it is safe to stop a car there at will. Yet of course cars barrel along those roads at 90 km/h (56 mph) or more, and a driver may not always realize that the car up ahead is not moving until it is too late. They may then try to swerve to avoid it, right into oncoming traffic.

This is bad enough in the summer when it is bright outside, but people do the same thing in the midwinter darkness—stopping on the road or on the shoulder so they can take pictures. I am sure I don't need to spell out how insane that is—a car without lights, parked on, or on the shoulder of, the country's main highway *in the dark*, with people perhaps wandering onto the road, absorbed in looking up or photographing the northern lights. Suffice it to say that people have been killed under those precise circumstances.

Bottom line: If you must take photos, be extra careful of your surroundings, and don't *ever* stop your car on the road. Use designated stopping areas or access roads for that.

Watch your step in geothermal areas

As you probably know, Iceland has abundant geothermal heat. In some places, in fact, so abundant that the heat that normally stays below ground bubbles up to the surface, creating hot springs or fumaroles—seething cauldrons of clay or mud.

Some locations with these natural phenomena are better known than others. Like, say, the Geysir area, which draws the greatest number of tourists of any site in Iceland. There you get both erupting geysers and bubbling fumaroles, and because of the sheer number of people who visit, measures have been taken to protect both visitors and nature from each other.

But not all areas are like that, and where there are no ropes or fences it is up to you to ensure you don't step into a hole filled with boiling water or mud that within seconds will scald the skin right off your body. I am not joking. If you are unfortunate enough to step into a hot spring, *do not take off your sock* until you receive medical treatment. Some people are in such great pain that the only thing they can think of is to rip off their sock in an effort to cool down their foot. But in doing so they will almost certainly strip off all their skin.

Bottom line: Be especially careful where you step around geothermal areas. And where there are ropes, respect them—for your own protection, and that of the land.

Out driving

Yes, Iceland's landscape is treacherous, and there are dangers in both expected and unexpected places. Yet the most dangerous aspect of touring Iceland is not those hot springs, glaciers or rogue waves, but something far more commonplace: driving.

Iceland has very low population density—3.74 people per square kilometre when this is written in 2023. Building and maintaining an efficient road system obviously costs a few crowns, and hitherto the Icelanders have been, if not entirely satisfied, then at least reasonably content with their single-lane highways, gravel roads, and the mountainous F-roads that are generally only open in summer.

So here we are, merrily driving on our sub-standard roads and suddenly there is a tourist boom, resulting in far more cars on the road than ever before, including whole convoys of tour buses. This means increased wear and tear on roads that were already unsuitable for so much traffic, and that require more frequent maintenance if they are to be kept safe. Also, many Icelandic roads are not built for the volume of traffic that they are now experiencing. For instance, shoulders have been known to collapse when a tour bus has moved too far over to one side of a narrow road, in order to make way for an oncoming vehicle. Thankfully there have been no serious injuries to people under such circumstances, but there have been enough scares to make people stand up and pay attention.

A related problem is the limited experience of many folks when it comes to the driving conditions endemic to Iceland. I am speaking of driving in strong winds, winter driving, two-lane highways, gravel roads, and so on. Some of our visitors come from countries with a completely different transportation culture, in which their main motoring experience has been in driving simulators. They have virtually no practice in driving on standard roads, much less roads that are more dangerous than the average. The number of accidents and traffic incidents involving such drivers has reached the point that the trend can no longer be ignored, and there have been calls for stricter regulations to make sure drivers of all nationalities are properly equipped for driving in Iceland.

So the road system definitely needs a major overhaul. However, that is not an undertaking that can be completed overnight, and besides, it is entirely open to debate whether we want all those roads improved. More on that later.

For now, at least, we must accept the sort of road system we have, and try our best to make our visitors aware of the main dangers and risks of motoring in Iceland, so that we can all stay safe.

So what are the main perils of driving in Iceland?

Wind

A far more apt name for our beloved Iceland would be "Windland", because rarely a day goes by when it is not windy. And when that wind turns to gale, which happens frequently, it can blow cars right off the road.

There are certain areas of Iceland that are more prone than others to those sorts of treacherous winds. Most notably around the coast, and where conditions are created by mountain slopes that direct the wind downward. If you are driving such a stretch of road it can be extremely dangerous in a storm. And stormy conditions in any location are risky if you are pulling a trailer behind you. You would not believe how easy it is for the wind to grab one of those puppies and yank it right off the road, taking you and your vehicle with it.

Even more horrific are the sandstorms that can hit in certain parts of the country, most notably along the southern coast where there are large stretches of black desert and volcanic terrain. Volcanic rocks, while very hard, are porous and light, and in strong winds they go flying through the air at a velocity that can smash in all the windows of your car within minutes. Every year there are tourists who underestimate the power of the wind and head out despite warnings, or who simply have not checked the weather forecast and unwittingly get caught in such a storm. I am sure I do not need to elaborate on the terror involved in sitting out in the middle of nowhere, with no shelter, and heavy rocks being hurled at your vehicle until all the windows break. And even if you are lucky enough to escape breaking glass, the blowing sand will almost certainly strip the paint right off your trusted vehicle, lickety-split. Something you might want to keep in mind when deciding on the type of insurance to get for your rental car.

Bottom line: If you are touring Iceland by car, check the weather forecast and road conditions every day. Bookmark these sites: en.vedur.is for weather, and road.is for road conditions. Remember that you can start off in sunshine in the morning, and by afternoon the weather may have turned and you'll be in completely different circumstances. Oh, and in addition to the rain and shine forecast, make sure you pay attention to the wind velocity. If possible, speak to a local about the weather and your planned route, and if there is a storm warning in effect, definitely stay off the road.

Driving too fast or too slow

We all know about speeding. You shouldn't do it. Especially not on Icelandic roads, where the main highways usually consist of a single lane in either direction. With cars barrelling towards each other at 90 km/h, all it takes is a moment of distraction for disaster to strike.

But speeding is not the only cause for concern. Motoring along a single-lane highway below the speed limit can also be very dangerous. Before too long a procession of cars will form behind you and eventually someone will try to overtake. Many, many fatal accidents have happened on Icelandic roads precisely for that reason. Perhaps drivers misjudge distances and wind up slamming into an oncoming vehicle. Or they lose control of their cars, especially where there are gravel shoulders (read: in most rural areas), and are subsequently hurled right off the road.

Bottom line: No speeding. Keep your wits about you, and take care not to cross into the opposite lane. If you absolutely must keep it leisurely and drive below the speed limit, pull over regularly to let the cars that have gathered up behind you overtake.

Or, use your indicators

There is another system that we Icelanders use if there is a car driving right behind us that evidently wants to go faster than we do. It is this: 1) make sure there is no one coming towards you up ahead, 2) make sure you are on a stretch of road where overtaking is permitted, 3) put your indicator on like you are going to pull off to the right, 4) slow down slightly, 5) allow the car behind you to pass.

I am not sure if this modus operandi is exclusive to Iceland, but I do know that it confuses many of our guests, who often seem genuinely befuddled by this oddball driving procedure. And so, assuming you are that person: if you are driving along on a highway behind another car, and that car puts on its right indicator while at full speed, they are likely giving you a green light to pass them because it is safe.

A word of warning: you will need to use your own good judgment here. If someone puts on their indicator, even if they are on a highway, it is entirely possible that they are, indeed, planning to make a turn. A good indication of this is if they put on their brake lights, or slow down significantly. So even though they are giving you this signal, you need to make sure there are, in fact, no cars coming towards you up ahead, and that you are not misreading the signal from the driver in front.

Naturally you don't have to accept the invitation to pass, and if you don't, simply make sure you leave an adequate amount of space between yourself and the car in front. The fact that they have just invited you to pass probably means they think you are too close for comfort.

Bottom line: If you notice a car behind you that looks like it wants to overtake, you can help that driver by making sure no one is coming, and then putting on your indicator to let them know it is safe. Conversely, if you are in a car close to another in front, and that driver puts on their indicator, they may be inviting you to pass. You should always use your own judgment, though, to discern whether that is actually what they are doing, and whether it is, in fact, safe.

Single lane bridges

These can be found all over Iceland, and they are among the most hazardous aspects of the Icelandic road system. Some are only a couple of metres long, others much longer. What they have in common, though, is that just before you get to the bridge, the road on either side narrows down to a single lane, and only one car at a time can drive across. Some of the longer bridges, though, will have little meeting points where you can pull off to the side if there is a car coming towards you.

As you approach a single-lane bridge you will first see a sign with an image of a car and then below it a road narrowing. Sometimes there will be another sign above that one with a big exclamation mark. This is your cue to slow down.

If there are two cars approaching the bridge from opposite sides at approximately the same time, the car that gets to the bridge first gets to cross it first. That's the law. The problem is that when you are hurtling along at 90 km/h and see a car coming from the other direction it can be very difficult to gauge who will arrive at the bridge first. It may look like it will be you, and you will keep barrelling along, safe in the conviction that you'll have the right of way, only realizing too late that the other car has actually gotten there first and is halfway across the bridge already. In that case you had better pray that you have the time and wherewithal to slam on the brakes before you plough into the other vehicle in that narrow space that is the bridge.

Bottom line: Always slow down significantly when approaching a single-lane bridge. If there is a car coming towards you, remember that the one that reaches the bridge first has the right of way.

Loose gravel

Although most main roads in Iceland are paved, about half of all roads in the country are gravel roads. Driving on those can be tricky, particularly if you are not used to it. Even just two wheels on a loose surface can send to your vehicle skidding into a ditch, or worse. On gravel your car behaves differently than it does on asphalt, kind of like the automobile equivalent of stepping on a banana peel. You may not fall, but you'll definitely feel like you are slipping, and you need to exercise special caution so that you don't lose control. If you are driving a 4WD you might consider using the automatic 4WD setting, which will detect any slippage and switch your vehicle into 4WD mode for added safety if the vehicle is unsteady on the road. Just make sure you set it back to normal when you are off the gravel, since driving for long distances on pavement using that setting is not good for the car's engine.

Also, be extra aware that roads in Iceland can turn suddenly from pavement to gravel. You may be merrily driving along a paved road doing your customary 90 km/h when suddenly the asphalt ends and you lunge onto gravel that may or may not be full of potholes. Those are prime conditions for losing control of your car. There will be a sign before that happens, though, showing a paved road and above that a car with pebbles flying off to the side, with the caption MALBIK ENDAR (asphalt ends).

Less serious, but still a matter of consideration: driving too fast on gravel can send little pebbles flying into the side of your car or someone else's, causing nasty chips in the paint or even damage to the windshield.

Bottom line: Always drive more slowly on a gravel road, pay extra attention to your driving, watch for signs that a paved road is about to turn to gravel, and slow down.

Blind rises

This is where the road goes up over a hill and you can't see if there is a car coming from the other side. If there is, it may appear just as you reach the top when it is too late to slow down to avoid a collision. So look for the road signs: two cars coming from opposite sides and driving up a rise shaped in an inverted V. If you see one of those, make sure you slow down and keep well over to the right hand side until you are over the crest of the hill.

Bottom line: If you see a hill up ahead, look for a road sign informing you whether or not it is a blind rise, and take appropriate action.

Seatbelts and headlights

These are compulsory at all times in Iceland. Always use seatbelts, and if the headlights don't come on automatically (which they almost always will in newer model cars) make sure you turn them on before you hit the road (and turn them off when you leave the car).

Bottom line: Buckle up, and switch on those lights.

Traffic circles

Known as roundabouts in some parts of the world, these circles for regulating traffic are all over Iceland. However, just to throw some confusion into the mix, the Icelanders decided to use them differently than folks in most other parts of the world. This is the result of some "tradition" that evolved and eventually stuck. Needless to say, this can be extremely dangerous.

The main thing to keep in mind when dealing with Icelandic traffic circles is this: the inner lane of a two-lane traffic circle has the right of way out of it. So if you're driving along in the outer lane you may suddenly be cut off by a vehicle that comes seemingly out of nowhere (that is, from behind you in the inner lane) and is on its way out of the circle. If you are not prepared, you could very easily crash headlong into the side of said vehicle, and it would all be your fault.

Bottom line: If you are in the outer lane, slow down at each exit and check to your left to see if there is a car about to cut you off. Better yet: enter into the inner lane of the circle, that way you always have the right of way out of it.

Single-lane tunnels

Iceland has a few mountain tunnels, mostly in the east and north of the country. A few of these are single-lane tunnels that stretch on for several kilometres, meaning they consist of a fairly narrow piece of asphalt with just the rock walls on either side. These can be pretty terrifying for those not used to them (not to mention folks with claustrophobia—yikes!), especially when you encounter cars coming at you from the opposite direction. Fear not: at regular intervals there will be spaces marked with a large "M" where cars can pull off to the side to let oncoming traffic pass.

The trick here is knowing who should do the pulling over into the M space—in other words, who has the right of way. Full disclosure: many Icelanders have no idea, and somehow navigate through with an odd mixture of courtesy and impudence. But of course there is a rule, and the rule will be posted prior to reaching the tunnel in the form of a traffic sign with two arrows pointing in opposite directions. One arrow will be white, the other red, and *it is the white arrow that has the right of way.* So if you enter the tunnel from the "red" side, remember it is up to you to pull over into the M space so the "white" side can pass. Then again, even if you are red it may well be that the car coming towards you will pull over, in which case you just graciously accept and motor on.

Bottom line: Before entering the tunnel, look for the sign that tells you who has the right of way and drive accordingly.

Sheep on the road

Iceland has a lot of sheep, and those sheep roam free in the summertime, albeit within regional confines. Their owners obviously try to keep them far away from any and all traffic, but alas, sheep don't always follow the rules, or stick to their designated grazing areas. They tend to meander, and sometimes they meander onto roads.

From a driver's perspective this is tricky because sheep are kinda hard to prepare for. Chances are slim that there will be a big blinking arrow on the road pointing at the sheep and telling you to slow down. The more common scenario is that you'll be driving along admiring the scenery and BAM!—suddenly there is a sheep in front of you. Or worse, it will be off to the side, grazing in a ditch and hidden from view, until it gets scared by your car and runs out right out in front of it, because sheep are foolish like that.

So, you need to be on the alert for sheep. Generally you will find them on the roads less travelled (gravel roads and F roads), though technically there is nothing stopping them from grazing along Iceland's main highway, known as the Ring Road, if they feel so inclined, especially in the absence of fences.

If you spot sheep on, or close to, the road, I probably don't need to tell you that you *must slow down*. Don't assume they'll automatically move out of your way. If you slow right down and they still don't move (very unlikely), give them a wee toot of your horn; that should do the trick. If it does not, proceed very, very slowly, until they catch the idea that you mean business and haul butt out of there on their skinny little legs.

Now, here is something very important to note: many of the sheep you see in the summer will be ewes with their lambs. Sometimes she will have one lamb, but more commonly two. If the ewe runs across the road, the lamb is guaranteed to follow. Sometimes the ewe catches on to the car before the lamb does and makes haste across the road, and a moment or two later the lamb will notice. Unfortunately, that moment or two may be about the time it takes for the car to reach the spot.

Meaning lamb crosses road to follow mommy, car hits lamb.

Obviously what we want to avoid at all costs.

In the worst-case scenario, if you hit a sheep or a lamb, never, *never* just leave it there, even if it is dead. Either go to the nearest farm and report it, or call 112. You won't be charged with anything, since everyone knows that these accidents can happen. However, notifying someone is very important for a couple of reasons. First, the farmer needs to know that they have lost a sheep or a lamb. Second, if you have hit a ewe then there is probably a lamb somewhere that needs to be fed, and it will die if no one comes to its aid. If you have hit a lamb, then the ewe will have stores of milk that will need attending to, and this could potentially help another motherless lamb.

Bottom line: Always be on the alert for sheep on the road, and whatever you do, *do not hit and run.*

Wayward horses

Occasionally this will happen: you'll come upon a herd of horses blocking a road. This is not likely to be the case on one of the main roads (like the Ring Road) but rather on side roads, often near farms. I should point out that Iceland does not have wild horses, only domestic ones, yet sometimes fences will be inadequate and they can wander away from the fields in which they are kept. These horses can be very curious about you and your car, and may not be predisposed to get out of your way. If that happens, proceed with caution. Do not start blasting your horn, since any loud noise or abrupt movement can startle the group, with potentially alarming results. Instead, inch forward slowly so that they move out of the way, until you are through.

Another point to mention about horses. Say you are out somewhere and want to park the car and go for a hike. If there is a group of horses nearby, and they have access to where you want to park the car, do not park the car. At least not there. The horses love to lick the salt off it, and when they do, they will almost certainly damage the paint. As in: they will gnaw the side of the car until the paint comes right off, and that is generally not covered by insurance. So heads up.

Bottom line: Don't spook the horses with any loud or sudden movements, and make sure they don't have your car for a snack.

Winter driving

Driving in the summer in Iceland is one thing, driving in the winter is quite another. The weather is worse, and roads are frequently icy, making it extremely easy to lose control of your car.

Probably the main thing to keep in mind when driving in the winter is not to head out in a vehicle that is poorly equipped for winter driving. Small compact cars are fine if you are driving only in Reykjavík, but the moment you head out into the countryside you really need to consider if that type of vehicle is suitable. It may well be, but that will depend entirely on conditions and also on the weather forecast. It is far too common for tourists to head out in a Toyota Yaris or similar when a blizzard is in the cards, and wind up stuck in the snow, even on frequently travelled routes like the Ring Road.

The other thing absolutely essential if you plan to head out of the city in winter is to have studded tires on your car. This is especially true if you are driving a smaller model of vehicle. Studded tires provide far better grip than non-studded, and the last thing you want on a single-lane highway is to be skidding all over the road. Studded tires are not compulsory in Iceland in winter, and in fact there have been campaigns in recent years to curb their use, at least within city limits, due to health risks (they tear up the asphalt and leave small particles that lodge in people's lungs, ick). If you are heading out of the city, however, and conditions are icy, your rental car should definitely be equipped with studded tires. Any responsible car rental agency should ensure that this is the case, but alas, some are more responsible than others, and there have been documented cases of cars being rented with inadequate tires for winter driving.

All that being said, even studded tires are not a guarantee against slipping if the road is covered in ice, so you do need to exercise the utmost caution in such conditions.

Bottom line: Make sure your vehicle is safe and sturdy enough for winter conditions and always have studded tires on your car if you are travelling outside of the capital in winter.

Google fail

One thing that has become increasingly common with the advent of GPS and Google Maps is people attempting to take mountain roads that are closed for the winter, all because Google Maps judges that to be the shortest distance between two points. No one informs Google about closures in Iceland, so it tends to chirpily direct people onto routes that are way, *way* off limits in the wintertime. And even though said road will have a chain across it with a big sign that says LOKAÐ (closed) or ÓFÆRT (impassable), people will ignore this, navigate their way around the chain, and ultimately wind up hopelessly stuck and dependent on someone coming to their rescue. Once upon a time this would have been a task for the regional search and rescue team, but on account of the frequency of these cases they have stopped handling them. Now there is a specialized company that rescues travellers from situations like these, and you can believe that they charge you handsomely for their services.

Bottom line: Check the website road.is for the most up-to-date conditions. And always, *always* obey closure signs on roads, even if it means not obeying Google.

F as in roads

A few more words about roads that are only accessible in summer: the notorious F-roads.

The "F" in the name stands for *fjallvegur* which in Icelandic means "mountain road" (*fjall* = mountain, *vegur* = road). Basically these are highland routes, many of which are little more than rugged tracks, and the majority of which require at least a 4WD vehicle. The F-roads are only open in the middle of summer, and the date at which they open varies according to conditions at any given time. The reason they are only open at the height of summer is that in winter they are obliterated by snow, and in the shoulder seasons they are normally so muddy that they have more in common with quicksand than actual roads.

The F-roads are divided into three types, F-1, F-2 and F-3, that admit different sorts of vehicles. The best among them, the F-1 roads, are accessible to robust 2WD vehicles and up. The operative word here being "robust". You should never attempt to drive a compact car onto an F-road, for example. Generally there will be signs at the opening of the F-roads illustrating the types of vehicles that are able to travel that road.

Bottom line: Always pay heed to these instructions, and never take the chance of driving an unsuitable car onto one of those roads. It could cost you dearly.

Crossing rivers

If you are driving on those F-roads, you may very well come to a river that needs to be crossed. Please be aware that this can be extremely dangerous! A few years ago, a young couple on their honeymoon got their car stuck in a river, resulting in a tragic death that could easily have been prevented.

Also please keep in mind that no vehicle is insured against damage when crossing a river, so even if your life or limb are not threatened, the weight of your purse might be!

The first thing to consider when embarking on a river crossing is whether you are driving the right kind of vehicle. To cross a highland river in Iceland you need a 4x4, and if the river is deep or the water volume substantial, you will need one with a snorkel. The water level must absolutely not reach the air intake of your car, for that will cause your engine to flood and the car to stall.

Second, on reaching the river, assess its depth. If you can observe another vehicle crossing ahead of you, great. If not, wade into the river to see how deep it is. If it is too deep to wade, it is too deep to drive through. Never, *ever* just drive in and hope for the best.

Third, assess the riverbed. If it is muddy, it will be harder to drive through, and the risk of getting your car stuck will be higher. If it is rocky, it will be easier. Use your common sense to decide whether to proceed, or to turn back.

Assuming you have done these steps and everything looks good, put your vehicle into 4x4 mode and proceed slowly into the river at an angle. The front of your car should be facing slightly downstream to minimise the risk of water entering the engine. Do not stop while you are in the river, and do not change gears. Keep your car in the lowest or second-lowest gear for the duration of the crossing.

Always be mindful of the fact that water levels can change depending on rainfall or meltwater. A river that is safe to cross one day may become unsafe a day later—or it may be safe in the morning, but unsafe in the afternoon.

If at all possible, try to cross in the company of another vehicle, or vehicles. After all, there is safety in numbers. Also keep in mind that cell phone service in the Icelandic interior is not a given, meaning you may not be able to call for help.

Bottom line: Rivers in the Icelandic highlands should only be crossed with the utmost caution, in an appropriate vehicle, and ideally in company with others in a separate vehicle.

On, never off

Before I abandon the subject of driving, I must mention something very important: going off-road.

For some reason, a rumour has spread far and wide that Iceland is the Promised Land for folks who want to go off-road and tear up the landscape in a big-ass vehicle, just for the hell of it.

This is not true. I repeat: *not* true. Any and all off-road driving is strictly forbidden in Iceland. Our country's terrain is largely made of volcanic soil, which is very loose. Car tires leave deep scars in the landscape that can take decades, even centuries, to heal.

"OK," you may be thinking, "I get that I shouldn't drive on grassy plains or on that moss that the Icelanders consider so precious, but surely I can go off-roading on some of that black sand. I mean, it's only sand." Wrong again. That sand happens to be home to very sensitive vegetation that gets destroyed when it is ploughed through with car tires.

Just to be perfectly clear: off-road means anywhere away from a designated road, whatever the terrain. To drive the point home (no pun intended), Icelandic law stipulates that anyone caught driving off-road can and will be fined heavily. And getting caught today is a lot more likely than it was a few years ago. These days there are people trekking all over Iceland, and most of them have a video recorder (read: smartphone) in their pocket. In other words, everyone is a cop. Just ask all the folks who have been slapped with heavy penalties in the last few years because someone took a video of them having a good old time doing doughnuts in the sensitive landscape. Police could identify their vehicles, and by the time the offenders were on the plane out of Iceland they were a couple hundred thousand crowns poorer, thanks to their misjudged escapades.

And now let us take a few questions

There is a rather excellent Facebook group called Bakland ferðaþjónustunnar (roughly translated: "The Travel Industry's Support Group") in which Icelanders involved or interested in tourism discuss matters relating to the industry.

A few years back someone started a thread asking what sorts of questions tour guides and others had received from their clients. There were literally hundreds of responses, and I'm going to be shameless and filch a few of them to share with you. I think you'll agree that some of the questions are utterly priceless.

- What time tonight do the northern lights start? (asked in the summer)
- If I go further north, can I see them? (asked in the summer)
- How far above sea level are we now? (asked on Reynisfjara beach, south Iceland)
- How do you celebrate the 4th of July?
- Which American state does Iceland belong to?
- What is the best time of year to see both the northern lights and the midnight sun?
- Where do you live in the winter?
- Why don't you speak to someone about the disgusting smell of the water?
- What was that wall built for? (asked while walking down the continental rift at Þingvellir)
- Is Iceland a third-world country?
- Is there an evening cruise where we can have a three-course meal and sail around Iceland?
- What are you doing to minimize the likelihood of another eruption?
- What colour is the red lava?
- Why don't you serve local red wine? (asked in a restaurant)
- What do you do with all those horses?
- The tunnel over to Europe is only for trains, right?
- Why are there so many tourists here?

- Is this the sea or a lake? (asked on a whale-watching tour)
- Is it safe to bring babies to the West Fjords?
- Excuse me, are there other mountains behind those mountains?
- Why are there no umbrellas for sale in the stores—does it never rain in Iceland?
- Where can we book a boat trip to the Blue Lagoon?
- I saw a bird outside my hotel last night, what is it called?
- What time do they turn the waterfall off in the evenings? (asked at Seljalandsfoss)
- Does the waterfall also run during the night? (asked at Gullfoss)
- Can we take a bath in the hot springs? (no) None of them?
- How do you bury people in the winter?
- Why do you build the roads like this, is it so that people drive slower? (asked about the F-roads in the highlands)
- How many slaves died building this? (asked about the continental rift at Þingvellir)
- Is this glacier attached to land?
- Which came first, the moss or the lava?
- Are those horses warm-blooded? (asked about Icelandic horses that stay outdoors in the winter)
- Where can I find the Golden Circle? (asked at Geysir, and later at Gullfoss)
- Is it true that the northern lights are radioactive and that

you have to go to the Blue Lagoon within 36 hours to get rid of the radioactivity?

- What is the address of the waterfall? (Seljalandsfoss)
- Do Icelanders have washing machines in their homes?
- Where can I see the Norwegian lights?
- I heard there are hidden people in the rocks and mountains here, why is that, did they do something wrong?
- Is the grass green in the summer? (asked in the winter)
- Where can we see the running lava?
- How long does it take you to drive to Europe?
- Where can I find the wall from Game of Thrones?
- What restaurants can you recommend in this area? (pointing to the centre of Vatnajökull glacier on the map)
- Who made these rock pillars? (pointing at the basalt columns in Reynisfjara beach)
- What is the difference between a glacier and a fjord?
- How can you fish in the winter, isn't the sea frozen?
- Aren't there any volcanic eruptions happening right now? When is the next one?
- Do I need a permit to scatter my relatives' ashes from a boat under the northern lights?
- Where can I see the natives? (believing Inuits to be native to Iceland)
- Can I adopt a whale so it won't be hunted?
- Is there a hospital in Iceland?
- Where is the school in Reykjavík?

- Was that the circle around Iceland?
  (asked after completing the Golden Circle tour)
- How much dynamite was used to make this?
  (asked while walking down the continental rift at Þingvellir)
- How did they transport the lava here?
  (asked while walking to the entrance of the Blue Lagoon)
- How many letters are in the Icelandic alphabet? (33)
  What do you use all those letters for?
- What month is it now? (September) Oh, you also have September?
- Why do you celebrate New Year?
  It is an American holiday.
- Is it true that the iceberg that sank the Titanic came from glacier lagoon Jökulsárlón?
- Where do you get your oxygen from? There are no trees here. (asked on the way from the airport, where indeed there are no trees)
- Is the president still in jail after the bank collapse?
- So what is the government doing to fill up the holes in the ground caused by the separation of the tectonic plates?

No, honestly. You can't make this stuff up.

What tourists think of us

But not all questions are outlandish or hilarious. A while back, daily newspaper *Morgunblaðið* decided to investigate what different nationalities who visit Iceland tend to ask about. Essentially they asked four tour guides four questions about their clients, who were of four different nationalities. The questions: 1. what do your clients ask about the most, 2. what do they find most strange in Iceland, 3. what do they find most interesting in Iceland, 4. what do they complain about the most?

We Icelanders hear a lot about what locals think of tourists, but not so much about what the tourists think of us. So for us this was both illuminating and refreshing.

Spanish tourists

They ask about: the cost of buying an apartment in Iceland, wages and taxes for normal people, health care and education, and what the main industries are. Also, they sometimes ask when the northern lights will come out … even in the middle of summer.

They find most strange: that they rarely see old people.

They find most interesting: all the water everywhere—waterfalls, rivers, glaciers … and the geology: lava, tectonic plates, sands, volcanoes. Plus the magical light that is ever changing.

They complain about: sub-standard accommodation and the lack of cleanliness in some places.

French tourists

They ask about: the volcano that grounded all that air traffic back in 2010, and where it is located. Social affairs: how Icelandic society operates, and how Icelanders manage to survive darkness in winter and endless daylight in summer.

They find most strange: that Icelanders believe in elves and hidden people (clearly no one has set them straight on that old chestnut … more on that later). That there are no palaces or grand buildings, hardly any trees, and that children are left unattended and sleeping in their prams outside cafés.

They find most interesting: the stunning nature—glaciers, volcanoes, northern lights, whales. Also the beautiful women (their words), and excellent food in Icelandic restaurants.

They complain about: the weather, but then again (to quote the tour guide) French people always complain about the weather, even at home. Also, the high price of wine.

Chinese tourists

They ask about: housing, how much an apartment costs, and how much land costs. How children in the countryside manage to attend school, given the sparse population.

They find most strange: not seeing ice or snow on arrival.

They find most interesting: the beauty of the landscape, and the diverse sights they are able to see on a single tour. The purity of the air and water.

They complain about: beds in Icelandic hotels being too small.

American, British and Nordic tourists

They ask about: the seasons—how cold it is in winter, how warm in summer. In the winter, when the northern lights will appear, and how long they will last. Also the midwinter darkness, and how it impacts the Icelanders' mood.

They find most strange: the absence of mosquitos in Iceland, and the fact that beer was banned for decades, while hard liquor was not.

They find most interesting: the nature and landscape, and the sense of freedom. The fact that they feel safe, especially the women.

They complain about: the high price of alcohol, though the happy hour deals in some bars and restaurants help alleviate the pain somewhat. The long lines to use the toilets.

Some questions answered

Given that those questions are so common among visitors, I thought perhaps some of you reading this book might have the same ones. And being the good question fairy that I am I thought I would jot down a few answers, in case they might be of interest.

How much does an apartment in Iceland cost?

Depends entirely on where you want to buy, and the type and size of the property. The most expensive properties, not surprisingly, are in the capital area. As this is written, the latest figures (from 2022) reveal that a square metre (roughly 10 square feet) in and around Reykjavík costs nearly ISK 598,000 (USD 4,200) on average. Based on that, a 100-square metre (1,076 square foot) apartment would set you back nearly ISK 60 million (USD 418,000). That said, flats in the most expensive locations in Reykjavík, in and around the old city centre, would be priced substantially higher, whereas properties in the suburbs, like Hafnarfjörður or Breiðholt, would be lower. The least expensive properties nationwide are in the West Fjords, where a square metre costs around ISK 244,000 (USD 1,700). The West Fjords are beautiful, but quite remote, and parts of them can be difficult to access due to poor roads and heavy snows in winter, hence the relatively low property prices.

I should probably note there are some restrictions to foreigners owning property in Iceland. Residents from the other EEA countries are able to buy property as if they were locals, but others must make a special application to the relevant authorities. This law is designed to ensure that large sections of Iceland do not get snapped up by, say, a large multinational corporation, or a Chinese entrepreneur with dubious intentions (as per one high-profile case a few years back). And lest you wonder why EEA members are exempt, it has to do with regulations stipulating that all citizens of those countries are treated as equal, meaning we can travel, work, own property, start businesses and more in any EEA country, as if it were our own. Which is why a British billionaire was freely able to buy up all those salmon fishing rivers in the East.

What are wages and taxes like in Iceland?

Average wages in Iceland for full-time employment in 2021 were ISK 823,000 per month (USD 5,800), which to many people in Iceland seems inordinately high. No doubt that figure gets a substantial boost from the top earners, of which there is a considerable number, as wage inequality is common in Iceland as it is in most parts of the world. Around one-fourth of all full-time workers earned less than ISK 600,000 a month (USD 4,200) in 2021.

In 2023 there were three tax brackets: 31.45 percent for monthly earnings up to ISK 409.986 (around USD 2,860), 37.95 percent for earnings between 370,482 and just over ISK 1 million (some USD 7,000), and 46.25 percent for earnings exceeding that. Each individual had a tax free credit of roughly ISK 60,000 per month (USD 418) in 2023.

Please keep in mind that the USD calculations are based on the rate of exchange in January 2023. The exchange rate fluctuates and is therefore not exact. Online conversion sites can be found widely on the Internet for those who want more current calculations of those figures.

What are the health care and educational systems like?

Iceland has universal health care—pretty much. When we need to see a doctor we can choose whether to go to our primary care physician, or directly to a specialist. A visit to the former will set you back ISK 500 in 2023 (USD 3.50). Mind you, there is a chronic shortage of family physicians in Iceland, so if the matter is urgent (as in, cannot wait several weeks) a visit to a doctor outside of normal hours will be required, which costs ISK 3,100 (USD 22). Concerning the latter … as of January 2019 specialists have no contract with Icelandic Health

Insurance (a government body), so they can charge as much as they please. A common rate for a visit to a specialist is ISK 20,000 (USD 140), give or take.

In recent years, the Icelandic government has been steadily increasing patients' share in the cost of health care, specifically for tests, treatments, surgeries, and so on. If you are relatively healthy and have a decent and regular income, you're fine. But if you get sick things can turn grim pretty quickly. Horror stories routinely appear in the media about people diagnosed with serious illnesses who have been driven to bankruptcy in trying to fund their health care. Often you see appeals for donations on their behalf, launched by their relatives or friends.

So, universal health care in name—but not necessarily in practice.

As for education, Iceland has four levels: preschool, elementary, upper secondary and higher education. Children enter elementary school in the year they turn six, and education is compulsory until they are 16. The upper secondary level lasts three years, from age 16 to 19. Standardised testing is administered at the end of elementary school, and again at the end of upper secondary school. Iceland currently has seven schools at the university level, some of which specialise in fields such as arts or business. Around 36 percent of women aged 25-64 in Iceland had completed tertiary education in 2020, compared with 25 percent of men the same age.

What are the main industries?

Fishing and fisheries-related industries have traditionally been the largest export sector in Iceland. Aluminium smelting came next, though it was always dwarfed by fishing. Yet in recent years tourism has surpassed even fishing as Iceland's main industry. In 2022 it accounted for 40 percent of Iceland's foreign currency income, bringing in ISK 460 billion, compared with ISK 260 billion from fishing.

When can we see the northern lights?

The best time to see the northern lights is from late September to the end of February. For a few weeks before and after that period they may indeed be visible, but it is more touch and go. It is likely obvious to most people that the northern lights are not visible in the summer, since Iceland has perpetual daylight then and the aurora can only been seen when it is dark. But as evidenced by the previous two sections, many folks come to Iceland during the season of the midnight sun hoping to see the northern lights. Alas, they are always disappointed.

Even if you visit Iceland during the darkest part of the year, though, there is still no guarantee that you will see the aurora. Conditions have to be just right: skies must be clear, it has to be cold, and the aurora has to "want" to appear—meaning there has to be a release of particles from the sun's atmosphere to collide with the gases in the earth's atmosphere (the basic explanation for the northern lights phenomena). There are ways to predict the best chance of seeing the aurora, and northern lights forecasts are widely available online. So are apps that both predict sightings and help you to take aurora pictures on your phone. The best views of the northern lights are where there is no light pollution, so the most dedicated aurora hunters tend to head out of the city if there is a chance of seeing them.

A word of warning: be extremely careful if you decide to leave the city to view the northern lights. Do not park by the side of the road (and definitely not *on* the road), or wander out onto it with your head craned back and eyes fixed to the sky. In autumn 2016 a man on a northern lights excursion with friends was struck by a car while wandering on the highway, probably transfixed by the spectacle above and completely unaware of his surroundings. So please, stay aware and alert.

How do Icelanders manage to survive the darkness in winter and light in summer?

It is true that the winter darkness can feel a bit overwhelming at times. The absence of daylight can trigger Seasonal Affective Disorder, or SAD—undoubtedly the most apt acronym ever. This throws people's body clocks out of whack and can lead to bouts of low energy, lack of concentration, dampened spirits and/or depression.

I have found the best way to survive SAD is to make sure I take walks during the day to let some of that daylight hit my eyeballs. Using a daylight simulator light is also good—a lamp that exactly mimics the shade and brightness of daylight. Regular light bulbs do not manage this—evidently they are too dim, and the light rays are not the correct shade of blue.

As for surviving the summer—that's a piece of cake. Most Icelanders have energy in spades in the summer months and need a lot less sleep than in the winter. The light in the evenings—to say nothing of the amazing midnight sun—is completely magical. For anyone who has trouble sleeping in daylight there are window shades that block all light, or good old fashioned sleeping masks. I suspect those are mainly designed for tourists, though, because I have personally never met an Icelander who has trouble sleeping in summer. My pet theory is that the Icelanders have a genetic mutation that allows them to sleep in bright daylight, equally as well as in darkness.

How cold is it in the winter, and how warm in the summer?

People are often amazed to learn that the average temperature in Iceland in the winter is around freezing on the Celsius scale, or 32 Fahrenheit. These mild temps are largely a product of the Gulf Stream circling the island, which helps moderate the temperature. In July the average temperature ranges from 10 to

13°C (50-55°F). These figures can be a tad misleading, though, both because wind-chill is an issue (so it can feel colder than the thermometer says) and because the sun is very strong (so it can feel warmer than the thermometer says, especially if you are sheltered from the wind). If you are wondering about the type of clothing to bring to Iceland, the most important thing is good windproofing. Layers are essential, because the sensations of being hot or cold depend so much on the wind and the sun that you want to be able to remove or add layers, as needed.

How do children out in the countryside attend school?

In a country as sparsely populated as Iceland, and with the population drifting increasingly towards the capital, there are certainly issues with children attending school in rural areas. School buses are widely used, and in more recent years remote learning via satellite classrooms has become a lot more common. When it comes to upper-secondary school, most young people from rural locations attend boarding schools, or go to live with relatives in urban areas during the school year.

Do you celebrate Christmas?

We most certainly do! Though Iceland is fairly secular, the overwhelming majority of Icelanders define themselves as

Christians, though they are unlikely to call themselves devout. Christmas is a huge deal—likely because it is the festival of light, and light is something we Icelanders cannot get enough of in the middle of winter. Preparations for festivities begin with the Advent, four weeks prior to Christmas Eve, when everyone starts putting up string lights and other decorations. There are tons of traditions associated with Christmas in Iceland, which I won't elaborate on here because they would probably fill an entire book—and as it happens, I wrote that book! It is called *The Little Book of the Icelanders at Christmas*, and it may be purchased both within Iceland and through online retailers. So the answer to the question is a resounding yes!

Why are there no umbrellas for sale in the stores—does it never rain in Iceland?

Oh, it most definitely rains in Iceland, are you kidding me? However, traditionally the type of rain we get has been accompanied by strong winds. Only in recent years has Iceland begun experiencing the sort of rain you get abroad, where it just comes straight down from the sky, and is not perpendicular. So there is not a tradition of umbrella usage in Iceland for that reason—either your umbrella would be torn right out of your hands, or it wouldn't do any good anyway since the rain comes at you sideways.

Do I need a permit to scatter my relatives' ashes from a boat under the northern lights?

Short answer: yes. Or anywhere in Iceland, for that matter. Is there anyone who monitors whether you have obtained such a permit before you scatter the ashes? Probably not. But you didn't hear it from me.

HÓTEL ÚTSÝN
Best View in the
HIGHLANDS

TOURISM AND
THE ENVIRONMENT

Not so much green

Not so long ago, tourism was regarded as a green industry in Iceland, even among environmentalists. In those days Icelandic policy makers relied primarily on heavy industry to give the economy injections. In practice this meant pandering to large multinational corporations that sought to build as many aluminium smelters in Iceland as possible, on account of the country's supposedly green energy and—more importantly—the low, low prices that Icelandic authorities were peddling. How green Iceland's energy really was, and is, is highly debatable—but that is another discussion.

Environmental activists in those days focused primarily on fighting the construction of new smelters and the power plants required to operate them. Tourism, meanwhile, was something to be encouraged, as it did not involve the destruction of large swaths of land, or belch out big clouds of smog.

Back in those not-so-long-ago days, fewer than half a million tourists visited Iceland per year, which is a rather different scenario from today. Nowadays the tourist industry has morphed into something else entirely, and environmentalists are no longer treating it as a happy alternative to smelting. Instead they are furrowing their collective brows in concern, and increasingly turning their attention to the three main ways in which tourism impacts the environment: depletion of natural resources, pollution, and physical impact.

In this section I will write a bit about how Iceland is affected. This list is by no means exhaustive, and I reiterate that these examples should be taken only as an indication of the sorts of problems the country is facing when it comes to tourism's effect on Iceland's environment—and what they are doing to combat those problems.

Depletion through development

Iceland is a country rich in natural resources. We currently have plenty of water, fish in the ocean, and abundant energy—at least for local consumption. In contrast to many popular tourist resorts, especially in warmer climates, we do not suffer from water scarcity. Nor does tourism place a particular strain on local resources like food, energy or raw materials. In that sense, we Icelanders are fortunate.

Yet depletion of natural resources is not always about

tourists eating up the locals' food or taking all their water for their showers or swimming pools. It also refers to loss of land through development or other activities. And when it comes to Iceland, there are a few red flags flying at full mast.

Incontestably, Iceland's biggest draw is its nature. Pristine landscapes are becoming a natural resource of their own as they become increasingly rare. Iceland's landscapes, of course, are not only unspoiled, but also very unique. Many entrepreneurs, meanwhile, see no problem with sacrificing large sections of these landscapes for financial gain, even while they earn their money selling access to the same natural wonders they are so indifferent about protecting.

Take the Icelandic highlands, for instance, the wild and uninhabited heart of the country. This is an area of tremendous beauty and diversity, incorporating deserts, woodland areas, glaciers, mountains, stunning colour palettes, hot springs, and a vast, expansive silence. The highlands are one of the largest unspoiled areas in Europe, and as such should enjoy protection by virtue of their sheer rarity, if nothing else.

Our guests, naturally, wish to experience these extraordinary landscapes, and make long trips to do so. Yet how far should we go in accommodating them, literally speaking, in their quest? Should we, for instance, build hotels in the midst of the wild unspoiled expanse, or does that destroy the very uniqueness of the site that they come to see?

You may have guessed what I am leading up to here. This question was recently brought into sharp focus when it was announced that a hotel able to accommodate 342 people was set to be built near the Kerlingafjöll mountains in the central highlands. Kerlingafjöll is an area of extraordinary beauty, with bubbling fumaroles and hot springs, and stunning colours and textures in the landscape. For years it was relatively remote, meaning that the gravel road by which it is accessed—known as the Kjölur highland route—was bumpy and rather rough, and the available accommodation was rudimentary, consisting of a handful of mountain huts and a campsite. But now, developers want to bring the area closer to the people, as it were.

And what, you may wonder, is wrong with that? If the hotel is tastefully constructed, if it blends well into the landscape and utilizes natural materials from the region, why should it not go ahead?

A hotel of that calibre in the central highlands raises a bunch of concerns. It would require plenty of electric power, and while Iceland has energy to spare, there is the wee matter of getting it to the hotel. Initially there were concerns about large pylons lining the highland route, but in 2019 power lines were dug into the ground, which from a conservation standpoint is a marginally better solution than aboveground cables, even if it requires digging trenches into unspoiled nature.

Water is another issue. While fresh water is not likely to be a problem in the area, the disposal of water used at the hotel will be. This includes sewage, which will have to go into a septic tank, which will need to be emptied on a regular basis. Trash will also need to be transported out of the area. Both will require trucks driving to and from the hotel. This, in addition to the tourists who will need to be conveyed back and forth, will very likely elicit calls for a better road than the one currently in use. More on that momentarily.

Under normal circumstances, an environmental impact assessment (EIA) is needed for a construction project of this size in a sensitive area. What we are increasingly seeing, however, is entrepreneurs "salami slicing" their ventures—getting around regulations by dividing construction into smaller phases, each of which does not require an EIA because of its insubstantial size. This was the strategy of the folks behind the hotel in Kerlingafjöll, who were initially given the green light to go ahead with the first phase of the project. The Icelandic Environment Association, an NGO, appealed the decision, citing that the construction was, in fact, part of a larger project that would most certainly need an EIA. The Icelandic Environment Association won the case, and the ruling stipulated that construction had to be put on hold pending a comprehensive EIA.

Much water has passed under the proverbial bridge since those first plans were unveiled. The initial idea to build a luxury hotel was amended, and currently a resort incorporating a hotel, lodges, a restaurant, highland baths, a "glamping" area, as well as a regular campsite, is under construction. The National Planning Agency has deemed the project "acceptable", whereas the Icelandic Environment Association has expressed concerns about the impact on nature, particularly concerning sewage. The Environment Agency of Iceland, a government body, declared the area around Kerlingafjöll a protected site in 2020, and has begun preparing for an influx of tourists in the area by building viewing decks and boardwalks, and laying paths.

Although there are currently no plans to markedly improve the Kjölur highland route, one wonders what will happen with increased traffic to the area. As we have established, Icelandic roads are inadequate when it comes to coping with tourism traffic … but do we really want paved highways through our precious highlands? Roads like that are a slippery slope. By their very nature they invite more use, and more use naturally leads to the construction of service stations and rest stops. Those will have to be preceded by signs. There may even be billboards. And before long: bye-bye pristine landscape.

I mentioned salami slicing. That is exactly what has been happening with the Kjölur route over the past two decades or so, with the Icelandic Roads Authority stealthily making improvements to the road while keeping the sections small. Allegedly this is because funding has not been adequate for longer sections to be improved at once, but it also means that no EIA was carried out, even though the sum total of the project would most certainly have required one. The National Planning Agency has ultimate authority over projects of this sort, yet in the majority of cases the Roads Authority neglected to inform the Planning Agency of their activities. In this way the Roads Authority has made improvements to some 40 km of the Kjölur route over the last two decades or so, all without undergoing an EIA.

No doubt the Roads Authority would argue that they were simply making the road safer for travellers. Yet middle ground must be found, and one proposed compromise is that improved roads not be laid in a straight line, but rather with curves and bends. Tourism professionals are in favour of this solution as it will allow their clients a better view of the landscape, and environmentalists because it will reduce speed and help eliminate the feeling that people are on a highway. Indeed, one of the complaints levied against the roads administration is that the 40 km overhaul of the Kjölur road was in fact done in a straight line, which does nothing but facilitate more and faster traffic through the area.

The best scenario from a conservation standpoint is to make the highlands into a national park. That would afford it protection against development, and also power harnessing—something that industrialists have been pushing for, and environmentalists have been protesting, for years. Indeed, a movement for protection of the highlands was launched in the early 2000s with a number of high-profile individuals, including Icelandic musician Björk, campaigning for its inception. A bill to that end was finally introduced in parliament in 2020. Alas, while the protection movement enjoyed widespread backing while it was still an abstract idea, support began to wane when folks began to realise what was actually involved. Photographers were disgruntled that a protected status would mean numerous "no-drone" zones; 4x4 and motor rally enthusiasts that their opportunities for driving would be curbed; local councils that they would no longer have planning authority over certain sites, and so on. The bill proved so contentious that it did not even make it to the voting stage, and as this is being written, it is still pending.

Pollution and the demise of Lake Mývatn

Like any industry, tourism causes pollution. In the case of Iceland, the most evident manifestations are these:

Air pollution. Emissions from increased air travel, a proliferation of cars on the roads, tour buses and cruise ships. Also from a rise in the number of cars with studded tires, as these cause small particle pollution when they tear up asphalt.

Littering. People throwing their stuff around. Cigarette butts etcetera. Infuriating.

Noise pollution. Particularly in the centre of Reykjavík, with tour buses picking up and dropping off people, suitcase wheels on pavement, and more.

Marine pollution. Mainly from cruise ships, of which 75 docked in Iceland in 2022, with some 421,000 passengers on board. The pollution dumped into the ocean from cruise ships includes anything from solid waste (objects like paper, aluminium, glass) to sewage. As yet there has been little discussion of Iceland's ecosystem being adversely affected by marine pollution, though that does mean that it is not happening.

Visual pollution. Power masts, billboards and such spoiling natural vistas and views. See previous section.

Water pollution. We Icelanders pride ourselves on our natural drinking water, which is among the purest in the world. Yet in recent years there have been increasing concerns about tourism's effect on our groundwater. One discussion that arose a few years ago was in connection with a company that offers folks the opportunity to be lowered into the chamber of an extinct volcano. The site, located just east of Reykjavík, is somewhat difficult to reach, and there was talk of how visitors could more easily be transported there. One idea was to build a road, the only problem being that it would have to cross the main groundwater recharge area for Iceland's capital. If anything were to occur there, like a truck overturning, or an oil leak, it would have serious consequences for Reykjavík's water supply. Such accidents have, indeed, happened in other parts of the country, prompting discussions about the potentially adverse effects of increased traffic on groundwater.

Water pollution can also incorporate sewage, which is all-too well illustrated by the case of Lake Mývatn.

Mývatn is a lake of exceptional beauty situated in a volcanic area in north Iceland. It is a UNESCO World Heritage Site, listed for its unique geological and biological properties. The lake has a remarkably varied bird life, and a rare and very delicate ecosystem. Until recently this was one of only two places in the world where you could find Cladophora balls (the other being Lake Akan, Japan), also known as lake balls, a species of living algae that grows into fuzzy spheres 10-15 cm in diameter.

In 2014 scientists announced that the rare lake balls had disappeared from Lake Mývatn, as something had happened to the ecosystem of the lake to stop their growth. The culprit was determined to be bacteria that were proliferating in the lake as a result of sewage seeping from outdated septic tanks in the surrounding area. This, coupled with other disturbing incidents such as a collapse in the arctic char stock and the mass death of ducklings, led the Environmental Agency of Iceland to put Lake Mývatn on its "red list" of places whose environment is under immediate threat.

This measure came two years after the Environmental Agency had put Lake Mývatn on its "orange list", which meant that the ecosystem was already at risk and needed to be monitored closely. More stringent regulations were then set for the disposal of sewage in the protected area surrounding the lake. The small community around Mývatn has no modern sewage treatment plant, and had for decades been using septic tanks to dispose of sewage.

With the tourist boom, there was a rapid increase in hotels being built near Lake Mývatn. This was of deep concern to environmentalists, given the extreme sensitivity of the area and its ecosystem. One condition for the building permits of these hotels was that they construct their own sewage treatment plants, to ensure the protection of the lake.

A regional sewage treatment plant was also a dire necessity, but was completely out of the range, cost-wise, of the tiny municipality of Skútustaðahreppur, which is made up of only 470 permanent residents. The municipality therefore appealed to the government for help, and given the "imminent natural disaster" happening at Lake Mývatn, as one MP put it, the then-minister for the environment promised funding to the district, to help build the required plant and to save the lake.

So far, so sensible. But in February 2017, an investigation by Icelandic news programme Kastljós presented an alarming picture of the situation around the lake. One of the new hotels in the area, Hótel Laxá, had agreed to the abovementioned sewage measures and advertised itself as a green hotel, making much of its eco-friendly status. The investigation revealed, however, that sewage disposal at the hotel had been in shambles virtually since it opened in 2014. The sewage treatment facility had been left unsupervised and mice had chewed into the control boxes, rendering it non-functional. Sewage, effectively untreated, was being disposed of into the delicate ecosystem of Lake Mývatn, and had been for over two years. The hotel's owners had been issued repeated warnings, but had done nothing to address the issue.

Things were not much better at another nearby hotel, Hótel Sel. In 2015 an annex was built onto an older building, doubling the hotel in size. The new building was subject to the aforementioned regulations from 2012 regarding sewage disposal. The owners of the hotel, however, had managed to secure an exemption on the grounds that they were waiting for the government-funded sewage treatment plant in the area to be built. A plant that had not yet even passed from the talking stage and onto any sort of drawing board. The exemption was made despite strong objections by the local health board.

Why was such a ludicrous exemption granted in the first place? Perhaps it had something to do with the fact that the district council is in charge of such matters, and the owner of the hotel also happened to be the chairman of the district council.

This was the situation in 2017, when the first edition of this book was written. Since then, I am happy to report, much has been done to improve the sewage-disposal situation around Lake Mývatn. In fact, it has transformed from one of the most alarming, to one of the most exemplary, sewage treatment solutions in Iceland. Indeed, no other municipality in the country is as advanced in sewage matters as Skútustaðarhreppur.

Essentially, what has been done is this: every company or institution in the municipality was given the option of setting up their own sewage treatment plant, or gathering the sewage into two separate tanks, a greywater and blackwater tank. For those who don't know (I didn't), blackwater is the stuff that comes from toilets and dishwashers, and greywater from sinks, showers, washing machines and such.

In the Mývatn area, blackwater tanks are emptied regularly, and their contents transported to an area nearby known as Hólasandur, where there is an ongoing land reclamation project. The sewage is treated with a disinfectant, then used as fertilizer on the area being cultivated. On the whole, the project is reported to be a great success, and indeed, a whole new subdivision in nearby Akureyri is now being constructed according to the same premise for disposing of sewage. After all, the blackwater waste is rich in nutrients, and with fertilizer becoming increasingly valuable and costly, using what is already at our disposal, so to speak, makes eminent sense, and is eco-friendly to boot.

Heeding the call

Then we have the sewage disposal conundrum in a slightly broader context.

Let's look at the facts: Iceland is sparsely populated, it has filled up with tourists at an unprecedented rate, and there simply are not enough toilets throughout the country to serve nearly two million visitors a year. In fact, in some parts of the country you can drive for hours and not see as much as a single port-a-potty, let alone a service station with proper facilities.

We who inhabit the land of ice have learned to live with this. If we have to travel long distances and know we won't be able to buy gas or food along the way, we fill up the tank and pack a lunch. When hunger starts to nag we find a suitable place to stop, preferably where we are sheltered from the wind, and have a little picnic. If it is raining we eat in the car. And if we have to serve the call of nature we serve the call of nature. Outside. In nature.

If we have to do number one, the business is relatively straightforward. If we have to do number two, we do number two, only we make sure it is covered with something when we leave. A rock, a piece of lava, some turf … whatever provides enough coverage so that no one will be unfortunate enough to stumble upon it, if you get my drift.

Now, all this requires a certain deftness in the disposal of toilet paper, when it is used. The number one rule is this: never *ever* leave bits of it just lying there on the ground. The wind will whisk it away—if not at this moment, then a few moments from now. And from there it can wind up anywhere. Understand? *Anywhere.*

Here is how we Icelanders have learned to do it: stuff the paper under a rock where it may decompose at its leisure. Or find a nook or crevice in the lava and shove it in there, making sure we close the space with a rock. If we happen to be hiking and the paper is relatively, um, clean, we use our hiking pole to stuff it deep into a crevice, or into soft ground.

Fast-forward to the present day. Hundreds of thousands of visitors touring the land, needing to heed the call. Suddenly, there is toilet paper *everywhere.* By the side of the road, along hiking trails, in woods surrounding picnic areas. White (and some not-so white) bits of paper lying, or even flying, around. Among trees, in the ruins of old houses, even in a flipping churchyard. Just lying there, waiting to attach itself to the underside of someone's shoe, or to fly into someone's food when they are having their lunch.

Seriously upsetting.

So who is to blame? The poor tourists who need to do their business? Icelandic authorities who haven't made enough toilets available for the poor tourists?

Well, we could play the blame game, but that's not terribly constructive. Yes, Iceland needs more toilets, just like it needs all kinds of infrastructure. But infrastructure improvements take time. After all, building a modern toilet facility is a complex undertaking. In a town or city it is not such an issue. Out in the middle of nowhere it is something else entirely.

Traditional toilets require both water and electricity. Many of Iceland's natural sites, located as they are out in the middle of nowhere, have neither. So new solutions had to be found. Currently there are new toilet facilities at Dettifoss waterfall in the north, and Askja in the interior, that employ the latest technology to meet traditional latrine requirements. Specifically, these are composting toilets, a type of dry toilet facility that creates a compost-like material out of human waste, that is subsequently used for revegetation in the area. Rather than laying electric cables, solar cells are used for power. Overall, a stellar solution to what for over a decade has been one of the biggest challenges relating to the tourism boom, that moreover makes a positive environmental impact.

We can only hope that the outcome proves so positive that such solutions are also implemented at other natural sites. Yet until that happens, potty breaks along some stretches of road in Iceland are bound to require some improvisation. If you are forced to use the great outdoors, I hope you will do as we locals do to help minimize the, um, pollution—or better yet, bring along your own poop bag, like they do on Mount Everest.

Getting physical

Now let's look at the physical impact of tourism. This includes things like construction, roads and amenities, degradation of marine areas, trampling of vegetation or sensitive locations, off-road driving, and more.

In Iceland we see all of these to a greater or lesser degree. Construction, as I have mentioned, is happening all over Iceland, particularly in the centre of Reykjavík, where it seems like every other new building is a hotel. There seems to be very little comprehensive planning in place, and older buildings are being torn down to make way for modern constructions of, shall we say, dubious aesthetic value.

Trampling of sensitive areas is a problem all over Iceland. Efforts are being made to construct boardwalks and paths at the most popular sites, but there is still a long way to go. In Iceland this is particularly serious because of the country's northerly climate, meaning that delicate vegetation can take decades, or even centuries, to grow back. Some tourists, evidently unaware of this, have even gone so far as to tear up large sheets of moss to pack around the bottoms of their tents for insulation. The next day they would likely have packed up and left, but the scars they created in the landscape will be there for another two hundred years.

Then there are the parts of Iceland that are systematically being removed, one piece at a time. I am speaking of pebbles and stones, some of which contain traces of minerals or precious metals—or not, yet which are beautiful nevertheless. Along the popular Laugavegur hiking trail there was once an abundance of obsidian—beautiful, glossy black stones that look permanently wet. Now there are hardly any left. They have been picked up by hikers, eager to take a natural souvenir home with them.

Similarly, at Helgustaðir in East Iceland there is a site where Iceland spar was once mined. Iceland spar is a clear form of calcite, a beautiful, transparent stone that has been widely used by the international scientific community to study the refraction of light. From the mid-17th until the 20th centuries, massive amounts of Iceland spar were extracted and exported. Mining at the site was stopped by the Danish government (of which Iceland was then a colony) in the late 19th century, but briefly resumed in the 20th. By that time, only a tiny fraction of the original mineral remained in the mine, and most of it was of a quality too inferior to be useful in scientific studies.

Not too inferior, though, to draw visitors to the site. They came to marvel at the crystalline formations embedded in the rock and alas, the temptation to take a piece home proved too great for some. With no guard on site, many took to illicitly removing the crystals, despite signs that expressly forbade it. The Helgustaðir mine is still open and accessible, and over the past several years, the spar deposits have been systematically disappearing. A warden of the site, who lives nearby but does not perpetually watch over it, has reportedly caught tourists with hammers and chisels heading down into the old mine, or coming away from it with chunks of spar in their pockets. A few years ago police intercepted individuals who were leaving the country with over 100 kilograms of Iceland spar. These days, only a few vestiges of the mineral left intact when the mine was closed still remains.

Right now, residents in the area who care about this natural gem are pressing authorities for funding to hire guards to patrol it. However, as with so many attractions in Iceland, the funding is not forthcoming—just another example of how Icelandic nature suffers due to poor planning, absence of policy, or lack of funds.

So please, remember the old maxim: Take only photographs. Leave only footprints. And kindly leave Iceland in Iceland.

Local authorities versus the state

Large-scale construction projects in Kerlingafjöll, at Lake Mývatn, and in other undeveloped areas raise a bunch of pressing questions. Such as: how much control should local authorities have over places that are of immense value to the entire nation?

Take the area around Kerlingafjöll, where the proposed highland hotel construction is set to take place. While it is part of the central highlands, it also happens to be within the borders of Hrunamannahreppur district in southern Iceland. Hrunamannahreppur has a population of around 800 people, yet the local council has the authority to grant permission for a hotel to be built that will have a major impact on its natural surroundings.

The 470-strong community around Lake Mývatn has similar authority over the area surrounding the lake. As we have seen this can easily breed corruption and mismanagement, as when the chairman of the local council is made exempt from regulations intended to protect a very delicate ecosystem.

The environmental impact assessment, of course, is designed to protect nature and sites of significant geological value. But, as we have seen, tricks such as salami slicing are used to bypass the assessment, allowing greed and profiteering to prevail at the cost of the environment.

Which begs the question: where are the regulators? With the Kjölur route, the Roads Administration got away with its own agenda for a full 20 years before anyone got involved. At Lake Mývatn there were three public bodies—the local health authority, the Environment Agency of Iceland, and Skútustaðahreppur district—that were supposed to monitor the situation around the lake. All failed. Rather than step in with authority and take charge, officials did nothing except write letters and send feeble warnings. When the news of the mismanagement at Lake Mývatn broke, each authority pointed the finger at the other.

Sadly, this is far, far too common in Iceland. The social fabric is too closely knit and nepotism and cronyism are rampant. No one wants to rock the boat, and those who push and manipulate the hardest tend to get away with shameless activity.

The state versus local authorities

The grave situation at Lake Mývatn is not the only one where Icelandic authorities seem completely out of their depth. There are a million other issues that need addressing and problems that must be resolved. Infrastructure needs to be developed, law enforcement stepped up, education increased, information disseminated, the safety of tourists ensured, the protection of the environment given priority, and much more.

Many of the measures that must be implemented require funding. So where should that funding come from? Should a tax be placed on tourists? Or is tourism generating enough income for the Icelandic state to fund infrastructure improvements and such without the direct involvement of its visitors?

As authorities debate this, a related issue crops up: who should get to dip their ladle into the pot of tourism revenues? Currently the state receives almost all the taxation income from our foreign visitors. It levies value added tax on goods and services, and given that the number of visitors is now around six times greater than the country's permanent residents, the greatest portion of those taxes come from our esteemed guests.

Local authorities, meanwhile, primarily receive their income through municipal taxes levied on the residents of their community. Yet they must also meet costs associated with increased tourism, such as garbage removal, cleaning of streets and sidewalks, building toilets, maintaining roads and facilities, and so on. The fact that they are not receiving revenues from tourism while providing a host of services has long been a thorn in the side of municipal authorities in the City of Reykjavík, for example. The capital, after all, is the gateway to Iceland through which most tourists pass, usually spending at least a few days.

Similarly, in the case of Lake Mývatn, it is easy to see how a district of 400 permanent residents does not have the financial resources to build a state-of-the-art sewage processing plant. In such cases it seems only fair that the state should step in to help fund the project. Yet if they do, should they not have some authority over the site that they are helping to protect? Which raises yet another in the endless string of questions posed by Iceland's new world order: whether the state should claim ownership of Iceland's most valuable and precious natural sites, ensuring that they become the property of the nation and thus affording them the necessary protection and conservation.

Taxing tourists, or not

I mentioned the tourist tax question. It has received a great deal of attention, both within Iceland and abroad, and has been the subject of much debate. Many folks feel that some form of tourism tax needs to be implemented to help provide funds for needed improvements, maintenance and safety measures. Among the main advocates of this are often the tourists themselves. They say they would be more than happy to pony up a nominal fee on arrival or departure from Iceland if it meant that the funds were being used to protect Iceland's nature, educate visitors about responsible tourism, or build up needed infrastructure in some way. In fact, many people are perplexed that such a fee is not already being applied.

Before I embark on the tourist tax discussion, I should mention that the Icelandic government does have a fund earmarked for developments in the tourism industry. Local authorities and individual parties can apply for allocations from the fund in order to build up facilities, strengthen safety, and implement other needed changes. Yet the fund is not inexhaustible, and individual allocations do not cover such areas as medical services, policing, and other factors that are the direct responsibility of the state, and which are increasingly under strain due to the influx of visitors.

The tourist tax question is somewhat of a heated topic in Iceland and has been discussed back and forth ad nauseam, with no real resolution. Some people, primarily Icelanders, maintain that tourists are already adding plenty of money to the national coffers—in other words that the struggle to cover costs is not due to a lack of funds, but to the way the funds are managed. If a more fair distribution of the wealth could be ensured, they argue, then there would be no need for a tourist tax. Yet that is a separate discussion, which veers rather sharply into politics and which I shall, for that reason, avoid on these pages.

So why is a tourist tax not being collected? Well, it turns out that this is far more complex than simply setting up an admission booth at the airport and having everyone pay. Four potential methods for collecting a tourism tax have been outlined; here is a brief rundown of the main proposals and their inherent problems.

Arrivals tax. This would be collected either as a border tax, similar to the ESTA or ETA fees collected on entrance to the United States, Canada and elsewhere, or as a surcharge added to plane tickets.

Problematic because: Iceland is party to the European Economic Area (EEA), as well as the Schengen "no borders" agreement, and both of those forbid the collection of a border tax. The leaves the option of adding a surcharge to plane tickets; however, this would require the same charge to be added to tickets on domestic flights, since the EEA agreement stipulates that passengers on international flights cannot be subject to surcharges not levied on domestic flights. An added tax on domestic airline tickets would indubitably cause a massive outcry among the Icelandic people, who already pay an outrageously high fee for flying domestically (it is cheaper for Icelanders to fly abroad than to fly within Iceland), and who moreover would take serious exception to being taxed for travelling within their own country. So this source of funding is pretty much out of the question.

Nature pass. A pass that visitors would have to purchase and be prepared to show if they wanted to visit natural sites that come under the nature pass scheme. Funds collected would be funnelled back to the sites that are a part of the scheme, so they could provide better infrastructure and services than locations that do not participate. The logic being that people would choose sites with good infrastructure over sites with no infrastructure. Nature pass holders would not always be required to show their pass on entry, but there would be random checks, and fines levied on people who were found not to hold a pass.

Problematic because: Setting up the scheme and its enforcement is both complex and expensive. Moreover, as the purchase of the pass would be optional and only certain sites were a part of the scheme, it is likely that many folks would shun the idea altogether and instead seek out locations that were not participating, and therefore not as developed. Those sites would then be exposed to greater damage than before. So the whole point of the scheme as relating to nature protection and conservation would be moot.

The nature pass scheme was introduced as a bill in parliament in 2014 and was, in a word, demolished. Not due to the glaring flaw concerning the protection of natural sites, but because MPs saw red at the suggestion that they would have to pay to visit sites in their own country. Cries of "over my dead body!" and "I'll go to jail first!" resounded, echoing the sentiments of many an Icelander whenever this idea is broached.

So why not simply make Icelanders exempt? Alas, not possible under the EEA agreement. One of its directives stipulates that there shall be no discrimination of any EEA citizen over another. That would mean that if EEA citizens were to be charged to visit certain sites in Iceland, Icelanders would also have to be charged.

To many of our guests, paying to visit a natural site in one's own country does not seem like a huge deal. They are used to it from back home, and fail to see the problem. Not so with the Icelanders. Until now, Icelandic law has stipulated that anyone is free to move anywhere in Iceland, provided they are respectful and do not cause damage to nature. Mind you, this excludes private land where entry has been expressly prohibited via "no trespassing" signs or similar. So the mere suggestion that we Icelanders might have to pay to visit, say, Gullfoss or Jökulsárlón, is enough to send even the most composed individuals into a fit of rage. Folks are particularly sensitive about Þingvellir National Park, which is a sacred place for many Icelanders. In 1930, the Icelandic parliament passed a declaration that Þingvellir should be "a protected national shrine of all Icelanders" due to its historical importance and unique geology. The thought that Þingvellir could be removed from the jurisdiction of "all Icelanders"—effectively taken away from the collective Icelandic population—is exceedingly traumatic for many people.

So despite the government's campaign and effort on behalf of the nature pass bill it was eventually thrown out of parliament, and even the minister of industry, who was responsible for its creation, conceded that it had been deeply flawed from the get-go.

Charging admission to individual sites. Just as it sounds. A tollbooth next to every waterfall, glacier, hot spring, geothermal area, lake … you get the picture.

Problematic because: Folks would have to be constantly pulling out their wallets. Like, every ten meters or so, because Iceland sure has enough beautiful sites that could warrant an admission charge. Obviously this would get pretty annoying. Also, all those admission booths and fences would be a major blight on the landscape and could severely damage Iceland's image and reputation. During the high season there would be long lines to enter, and who wants that? People would inevitably start to avoid places where they had to pay, seeking out other sites where there was no charge, and also no infrastructure. Ergo: destruction of vulnerable nature. Also, many natural sites are privately owned, so the fee would go straight into the pockets of the landowners rather than into the collective fund reserved for protecting natural sites. And from an exclusively practical standpoint, this would be the costliest method by far of collecting a tourist tax.

Aside from that, if private landowners were to charge admission to their own land, it raises a bunch of issues concerning their associated responsibility. Say a tourist was injured while visiting a site on private land for which he or she has paid to enter. Naturally it would follow that the landowner was liable.

That landowner would therefore need to buy insurance for such eventualities. There would also have to be facilities such as toilets in place, the site would have to be developed so that it was as safe as possible for visitors, and its natural surroundings protected. Pretty soon, every other site in Iceland would be developed, and the country would have lost its "unspoiled" charm.

Brief addendum: a few years ago, private landowners whose sites were increasingly beset by visitors decided they couldn't wait for the government to get its act together on funding infrastructure improvements and measures for protection. So they started putting up fences and admission booths and charging people on their own initiative. This caused a major kerfuffle, especially in the Geysir area, which was jointly owned by private individuals and the state. The area, probably the most popular tourist site in Iceland next to the Blue Lagoon, draws thousands of visitors per day. In other instances where private owners had begun to charge, tourism companies rebelled and stopped taking visitors to those sites. However, they could not very well stop taking their clients to Geysir, which is one of the stops on the tremendously popular Golden Circle tour. Eventually the state took the private landowners to court and won, putting a stop to the admission charge and at the same time generating a lot of bad blood. In October 2016 the state finally bought out the remaining landowners, bringing the Geysir area entirely into public ownership.

Say what you will about the private initiatives of the landowners, their actions certainly served to highlight the necessity of doing something about the protection of natural sites throughout Iceland, and as such they should perhaps be thanked.

Accommodation tax. This form of funding means that a surcharge is added to the bills of folks staying in hotels or guesthouses. The advantage of the accommodation tax, and what makes it a favoured solution for many people, is that it bypasses all those pesky EEA directives and charges the primary users of the services that will be funded. Incidentally, as far as I can ascertain this is the same as the "city tax" or "hotel tax" charged in many cities across North America and Europe.

Problematic because: For revenues to be high enough to make a difference, the charge would have to be fairly steep. In September 2017, the accommodation fee was raised from ISK 100 to 300 per unit, yet it is still unlikely to be enough to cover the cost of all that needs to be improved. (Brief aside: the accommodation tax was temporarily suspended in 2020 due to the collapse of tourism during Covid, and will remain so until 31 December 2023.) Further, it is debatable whether it is fair that a tax on a single sector of the tourism industry—hotels and guesthouses—should be used to fund necessary improvements for the industry as a whole. To say nothing of the inherent unfairness of making hotel and guest house owners charge their clients a tax, while those who rent out Airbnb units or camper vehicles get away with not doing so. A situation that will eventually be rectified, surely, to be on par with cities like Paris, where Airbnb hosts are obliged to pay an accommodation tax to the state.

Given the above, you will surely agree that collecting a tourist tax to help fund infrastructure improvements is far from straightforward. As I explained there is strong opposition among the Icelanders to anything that might restrict them from roaming freely on their own soil, and no politician wants to be responsible for decisions that ignite such strong, negative feelings among the electorate. Even if everyone could rally behind a specific decision, there would still be endless debates on how to divvy up the pie, and what criteria should be used when allocating funds. Should it depend on the significance of the site? The number of people that visit? The need for facilities? Employment requirements in the community? The potential for argument is endless, and if anything is certain it is that no one will ever be 100 percent satisfied.

Reddast þetta?

With the myriad questions arising via the mass influx of tourists, and given that the tourist industry is currently Iceland's primary source of foreign exchange, it receives remarkably little attention from its elected officials. Or, if it does, it seems they do little more than flounder about, bickering about minor details while the big issues that urgently need attention pile up. Leading up to the elections in late 2016, the subject of tourism made barely a blip in the various debates.

When this is written in 2023, the Icelandic government still has no comprehensive, long-term strategy in place for either the growth or decline of tourism in the country. Iceland's leaders seem to treat mass tourism with the laissez-faire attitude so characteristic of the Icelandic people, generally exemplified by the ubiquitous phrase *þetta reddast*, meaning "it will all work itself out, so I'm not going to worry".

Which in itself is rather worrying.

FORSETI
EINKABÍLASTÆÐI

TOURISM AND THE LOCAL POPULATION

Ambivalent feelings

So what about the locals? How do Icelanders feel about all the tourists spilling into their country?

It is a question I get often, and it is not one that can be answered with a standard response, for the simple reason that "Icelanders" is not a uniform group. It is a group made up of individuals, each with their own subjective view of the matter, and each impacted in a different way. Some people are thrilled about the tourism boom; others are not so thrilled. Some are thrilled about one aspect of it, not so thrilled about another. Some are thrilled about it on Tuesday, ranting about it on Wednesday.

One friend lamented over dinner recently that she felt as though she had "lost her country" because all those semi-secret places to which she escaped in the past, and where she had almost always been alone, had now been exposed by travel books and invaded by tourists. This is a common refrain. Until recently we Icelanders were used to having plenty of space, to going wandering or hiking somewhere and not seeing another soul. Not anymore. Worse, often those secret hideaways and out-of-the-way places that we had come to love and regard as our own are not treated respectfully by people who have no emotional attachment to them.

I have a place like that: a certain waterfall near a cottage I used to go to every summer. It is off the beaten track, and from one side it is only accessible by a stone bridge across a river, after which you have to walk a ways along a trail that has been cut into a birch forest. The trail ends at a wide river that cascades down a set of cliffs roughly in the shape of a horseshoe. The water gathers below the cliffs into a whirlpool that over time has dug a deep hole in the riverbed, and which is the most exquisite shade of aquamarine. High up above that pool, perched on two cliffs on the opposite sides of the river, is an old bridge on which I used to sit and look down at the fresh, clean water as it swirled around in the whirlpool in a last twirling dance before it headed downstream towards the sea. I would sit there for long periods, watching the water rushing below the bridge, absorbed by the hypnotic sound it made, mesmerized by its clean, clear beauty. By the time I left I would feel simultaneously energized and infused with a deep calm.

The last time I was there, the first thing my husband and I saw as we emerged from the woods was two tourists picking their way over the shallows of the river just above the horseshoe cliffs, clearly unaware that if they lost their footing they might well be propelled down and into the deep whirlpool where they would probably drown. We waved our arms and shouted to them to turn back, that what they were doing was dangerous. They did turn back, and met us on the bridge that they should have taken across in the first place, where they informed us in a fairly curt manner that we were likely wrong, and that they probably could have crossed if they had continued on.

Tragically, this very thing happened in the summer of 2022—a man leapt into the river, a little ways down from the falls, in order to save his son; he was swept away, and drowned.

Not that the crossing or not crossing of these people was any of our business. And it is not like they were doing anything specifically disrespectful—they weren't throwing their cigarette butts around, or litter on the ground, as I have witnessed in other locations in Iceland. It's just that … I don't know, the energy is bad. It's hard to explain, and probably I shouldn't even be whining about this because, well, tourism saved our economy, and I am reaping the benefits like most of my countryfolk. But then again, some things just feel *wrong*. It's complicated.

How to piss off a local

But not all tourists exude the wrong kind of energy. In fact, one of the more frequent questions I get from people about to visit Iceland is how they can be "good" tourists. Which I take to mean: *how can we be respectful visitors and not piss off the Icelanders?*

First of all, it is inspiring and uplifting to discover how many people are concerned about this. I am delighted that there are so many folks out there who want to travel responsibly and in harmony with nature and with the locals. Those are the sorts of visitors we like to welcome to our country.

And yet it must be said: there is a growing discord among the Icelanders when it comes to tourism, an irritation about certain things. The sheer number of people everywhere has something to do with it, but there are also specific behaviours that upset and annoy the locals. Some may be attributed to cultural differences or simple misunderstandings, whereas others seem to stem from blatant disrespect.

One problem, of course, is that the perpetrators of the annoyance (the tourists) are often not aware of the effect their behaviour is having. They are just merrily carrying on, oblivious to their gaffes or the furrowed brows of the nearby Icelanders. In some cases they think they are showing goodwill or respect when in fact they are aggravating the hell out of the locals. And therein lies the difficulty: the locals moaning and complaining in one corner, the happy and carefree tourists in the other, and no real dialogue in between.

Well, help is on the way for those of you who want to be good and responsible tourists. Here are a few of the things likely to get up the Icelanders' nose that you might consider doing, or not doing, if you want to be in their good graces.

Not showering naked at the pool

This is probably *the* single biggest offence that any foreign national can commit against the Icelandic citizenry as a whole.

If you have been to Iceland you will know that pretty much every community throughout the land has its own swimming pool. This pool is the locals' community centre—where we go to meet up, decompress, exercise, play with our kids, sunbathe in warm weather, sunbathe in cold weather, exchange news and views, debate politics, and more. The pool is our English pub, Parisian café, Turkish teahouse. It is our oasis.

To visit this oasis, folks need to observe some ironclad rules, mostly to do with hygiene. The top one, and the one that every Icelander obeys, is this: *you must shower without a swimsuit before entering the pool*. It is non-negotiable. You gotta do it. And by "shower" I do not mean hurriedly ducking under the waterspout for five seconds before jumping into your swimsuit and heading out to the silky warm embrace of the pool. It means lathering up all your bits with soap, including, and especially, your private bits, and then rinsing thoroughly until you are clean.

For us Icelanders, this ritual is second nature. We are trained in it from infancy. Being naked in the shower with strangers is a total non-issue for us. Granted, most of us have developed a certain skill set for washing whereby we turn ever so slightly away from the next person as we lather and rinse. It is discreet and thorough at the same time. And nobody stares because nobody cares. That is, unless you break ranks and don't wash properly—that is when people will really notice.

This "properly" starts with not wearing your swimsuit in the shower. Seriously: how are you going to wash thoroughly with your swimsuit in the way? You can't.

Folks who are uncomfortable with this procedure may be tempted to cheat and do a "quick rinse", ideally while keeping their swimsuit on. But make no mistake: if the shower police (aka locker room staff) catch someone "washing" with their swimsuit still on they will stride over and order the delinquent guest to get their kit off and wash pronto—in front of everyone. And you best believe there will be some serious staring then.

See, we Icelanders like our pools clean, and preferably free of chlorine. We have a trust system, and that trust assumes that no one gets into the pool with their nether regions and other relevant parts unwashed. And no, it is not enough to have showered in the morning, or the evening before, as some people like to argue. It has to be done *at* the pool, *in* the shower, immediately before getting in the water, otherwise it doesn't count.

Tourist cairns

In the old days, before there were GPS and smartphones and Google maps, the Icelanders had to navigate the countryside in all sorts of conditions. Among the most dangerous of those was fog. It could persist for days, and if you got caught in it you were in big trouble. You could easily wander around blindly until you collapsed from fatigue, or hunger, or hypothermia. Either that or it would obliterate your view of the dangers up ahead, like that a cliff edge you might fall off, or deep crevice in the lava that could easily swallow you whole.

So to help people navigate, folks would stack cairns on the various trails to act as guideposts. These cairns are still visible in many places throughout the land, though they no longer serve any specific function.

Now, for some incomprehensible reason, tourists have begun to stack their own miniature cairns all over the country. Not for navigational purposes. Apparently … just because. This drives the Icelanders bonkers. When there was only the odd small cairn here and there, it was no big deal. But when they started appearing everywhere they became like the visual version of nails scraping along a blackboard, sending a shudder of AAAARGH through your body.

A discussion about this irritating practice appears every so often in my aforementioned favourite Facebook tourism group. There it is plain to see just how much the Icelanders hate this behaviour. People even make plans to go out together to locations where they know there are cairns for the sole purpose of destroying them. Some places in Iceland are more likely than others to have these offensive protuberances appear … one tour guide reported that some 80 to 100 tourist cairns (which is what the Icelanders call them) had been spotted in the Kaldidalur area in west Iceland. The road to Þingvellir via Mosfellsbær also seems to be a serious target for some reason.

As if this were not provoking enough, this strange cairn fixation seems to have taken on a life of its own, removed from all rhyme and reason. Recently I came across a picture on the Internet that a visitor had posted of a tourist cairn, captioned: "An elf temple". *What?* Seems that the elf myth has become intertwined with those stupid cairns, although the two have nothing, I repeat *nothing*, to do with one another.

So please. Lay off the tourist cairns. They're not contributing anything of value and just make for unsightly warts on the landscape.

Coins in hot springs or practically anywhere

Go to Europe and you'll see folks throwing coins in fountains to make a wish. Come to Iceland and you'll see folks assuming that the same rule applies, and tossing metal coins into hot springs or any body of water, large or small, that they deem appropriate. People: there is no tradition of coin tossing in Iceland, save for in one place. That place is Peningagjá, literally "Money Ravine", at Þingvellir. The practice there began in 1907 when a bridge was built over the ravine near the church site, and people began throwing coins into the deep rift. Over time it became a symbol of the value of the fresh water filling the ravine, and in fact it looks rather beautiful, with the silver glittering in the crystalline water. So if you must throw coins, please refrain from doing it anywhere else but there.

Freeloaders in camper vehicles

Accommodation in Iceland is expensive. It is also scarce, in the summer at least. Mix this with the fact that tourists want to be on the move in Iceland to experience all that stunning scenery and you come up with a pretty stellar business idea: camper vehicles—small vans equipped with beds and the equipment you need for basic cooking.

Vehicles of this kind have grown exponentially on Iceland's roads since they first started appearing around 2012. In high season they are everywhere, and as such, they aren't bothering anyone. The problem starts when the people who rent them think they can sleep anywhere, serve the call of nature wherever it is most convenient, shower in hostels where they haven't paid to stay, and park outside any establishment with Wi-Fi so they can surf the web at their leisure.

Not everyone in camper vehicles is so uncouth of course, but there are still enough to make some Icelandic hostel and guesthouse proprietors seriously lose their cool. And who can blame them? Here they are trying to run an establishment that only makes money a few months out of the year (if they are located outside the capital area, at least), and people keep taking advantage, or even freeloading, off their services. Consequently camper vehicles have got a pretty bad rap, and even people who wouldn't dream of filching an illicit shower are regarded with suspicion and even derision.

Sleeping anywhere

In related news, people who rent said camper vehicles have been known to stop in the unlikeliest of places in order to bunker down for the night.

To be fair, the companies that rent the vehicles can be held at least partly responsible for the ill-advised behaviour of their customers, as their promotional campaigns in the past have often condoned and even urged this sort of irresponsible conduct. When more and more complaints started trickling in, and that trickle turned to a steady stream, they clearly saw it was to their advantage to mediate their message somewhat. Hence people are no longer urged to sleep "anywhere" in their camper vehicles, which is just as well because in July 2016 new bylaws were passed prohibiting overnight stays of all kinds outside of designated camping areas, unless the landowner has expressly granted the intrepid campers permission.

Such permission had most certainly not been granted to the two young ladies who pitched their tent next to the upscale road Ægisíða in Reykjavík around New Year's (yes, in the freezing cold), or the tourists who pitched a tent in the yard of the historic Höfði House in Reykjavík, or the people who put up a tent in a private garden in Vík, which the homeowners discovered upon returning from holiday early one morning. It was *especially* not granted to the British couple that in August 2016 decided to park their RV in the parking lot of Bessastaðir, the official residence of Iceland's president, for a cosy overnight stay. And before you ask, Iceland does not have fences or security around their president's residence; however, that does not mean it is open to complete strangers who decide they want to camp out in his parking lot.

Two things are needed. One, some consideration from our guests, to stick to designated places for sleeping. Yes I know it is tempting to park that camper out by the Grótta lighthouse, the westernmost point of the Greater Reykjavík Area, where the Icelanders go to watch the sunset or walk their dogs. Sometimes there are up to ten vehicles out there, making it more akin to a trailer park than a place for a romantic stroll. Two, we need to get some law enforcement on the case, people who are not reluctant to slap offenders with fines. Because, really, it's trespassing on our common space, and not likely to earn visitors any points with the locals.

Don't pet the horses

Icelandic horses are adorable, aren't they? So small and cute, and fluffy in the winter. Great to take a selfie with. In fact they're such a hit that bypassers, and even Icelandic tour operators, have taken to stopping cars or whole buses by the side of the road so that people can get out, pet the horses, and take pictures. Harmless, right?

Actually, no. Most horse owners are super annoyed that their horses are being used as sightseeing attractions. Think about it. Every day people are stopping to schmooze with your horses and feed them treats—some of which are outright dangerous to the horses' health—without your permission or even your knowledge. They are turning your horses into pets. Meanwhile you may be in the midst of a rigorous training programme with your steeds and feeding them treats only when they perform the thing that you are trying to teach them. Except now they're getting treats simply by standing there and batting their eyelashes at people, which totally interferes with all your work.

Let us further assume that one of your horses is having an off day, flies off the handle, and maybe bites someone. Or, a tourist enters the corral or field where the horses are kept (happens) and that same grumpy horse gives them a nasty kick, potentially injuring them. Who is liable? You, the owner, because the injury happened on your land? These are the sorts of questions many Icelandic farmers are pondering right about now.

One farmer, whose horses graze on land that lies between Gullfoss and Geysir, two of Iceland's most-visited tourist attractions, was exceedingly tired of up to twenty vehicles at a time stopping by the side of the road and tourists then "emptying their cars" of anything they thought his horses might possibly eat. But rather than merely fume and rage, the farmer, to his credit, decided to take a constructive approach to the problem and set up a special corral with selected horses to greet tourists. The corral is located next to the road, and the farmer has even constructed a parking lot where cars can stop, which vastly improves safety. The farmer's hope is that by trotting these selected steeds out as a meet-and-greet committee, his more vulnerable horses will be left in peace. The only condition he makes is that visitors do not feed them any of their own food. Instead he has set up a booth with small cartons of feed for guests to purchase on an honour system for a nominal fee, which also helps him offset some of the costs of his little venture. An excellent initiative if you ask me, and one that bears supporting. So if you are travelling the Golden Circle and are in the mood for some horse canoodling, keep an eye out for the corral, located some 2 km east of Geysir (en route to Gullfoss), and make sure you bring some spare change for treats. Otherwise, if you must stop and pet a horse, consider going to a horse rental or a horse farm that allows for that sort of interaction. And leave the other horses, the ones minding their own business behind that fence, alone.

Calling Icelandic horses ponies

On the subject of horses, here is something else (though rather less grave) that seriously irks the Icelanders: calling their horses ponies.

I know, I know. The Icelandic steeds are rather diminutive and ... oh all right, technically they *are* ponies. Still, the Icelandic horse is always *called* a horse—not only by the Icelanders themselves but also breeders the world over. What gives?

Well, one theory is that Icelandic has no word for pony, only horse, and therefore Icelanders have always looked upon their horses as horses.

Another is that, while the height of the Icelandic horse classifies it as a pony, its weight, bone structure and weight-bearing capabilities are actually more like that of a horse. Not to mention their temperament, hardiness and spirited nature, which is more akin to a horse than a pony.

So how about we agree on this: the Icelandic horse is a pony on the outside and a horse on the inside. And the Icelanders like to call it a horse because it is horsey, not pony-ey. And they would prefer that you do so, too. The end.

Failing to take proper precautions and needing to be rescued

Moving right along to a considerably more serious topic: tourists needing to be rescued. I am going to write more about Iceland's search and rescue teams in another section, but suffice it to say that they are loved and revered by pretty much all Icelanders for their selfless sacrifices and excellent skills, all aimed at keeping other people safe. The high esteem in which they are held is augmented by the fact that a) all Icelandic search and rescue people are volunteers, and b) they are responsible for securing their own funding.

Obviously no one gets pissed when tourists, or anyone for that matter, legitimately needs to be rescued. Accidents happen, and when they do it is comforting to know that the SAR teams are always standing by. What does get infuriating is when folks wilfully ignore warnings, or weather conditions, or their own common sense, and head out into situations they have no business being in ... and then need to call on other people to rescue them, with the associated resources and costs—financial, physical and psychological.

Like, say, the three dudes who set out to cross Vatnajökull glacier on cross-country skis in March 2015. A risky undertaking at that time of year, but whatever. Granted, they were not amateurs, they had proper equipment, and they thought they were well prepared. Except that in Iceland, "well prepared" is all relative. Within the first couple of days one of them fell ill and needed to be rescued. When the regional SAR team found the hapless trio they informed them that a storm was about to blow in and strongly advised the remaining two to get off the glacier. They even offered them a ride. The pair shunned their warnings, adamant that they would be able to handle it. Well, they couldn't handle it. Two days later they had to be rescued … by that same SAR team. Who now had to spend time, energy and funds to go up there *a second time*.

This is the sort of thing that infuriates the local population, for obvious reasons. I mean, come on. Those search and rescue people have jobs, families, children, commitments, and things that are important to them. They don't need to be sent out to rescue two reckless asshats who insisted "no no, we got this".

I know what you're probably thinking: make them produce the funds for their rescue. But ICE-SAR is strongly opposed to that idea, for reasons on which I shall elaborate shortly.

Displaced from the capital

The place where the tourist boom is probably most keenly felt is the downtown core in Reykjavík. Some things have changed for the better there, others for worse, but they have definitely changed.

Perhaps the most obvious alteration is that hotels and guesthouses have proliferated in the downtown area since 2010. These days it seems that a new hotel has been built approximately every ten metres. It's insane. And of course the question on everyone's mind is what is going to happen if the tourists stop coming—as, indeed, they did during the two years of the Covid pandemic. Some businesses in the tourism industry folded at that time, but most scraped by, largely on the back of economic measures introduced by the Icelandic government that helped stave off bankruptcies.

Journalists routinely shove microphones at local officials and ask them "when is enough, enough?" of hotels, at which they sheepishly admit that enough is probably already enough—they just haven't gotten around to doing anything about it. A few days later there may be a report that they are now absolutely, definitively going to put a cap on new hotel buildings in downtown Reykjavík, but then you hear of yet another being built and you shrug and shuffle past, muttering something about Reykjavík becoming the Nordic version of Benidorm.

In other words, the potential problems inherent in unbridled hotel construction are apparently being deferred to a later time. But residents of the downtown core are starting to flee. I consistently hear of people selling their properties and moving out of the city centre as a result of escalating tourism.

So what exactly are people fleeing?

It is not the foreign visitors per se. The overwhelming majority of visitors to Iceland are courteous and respectful, and mingle quite effortlessly with the Icelandic population. However, when it starts to feel like you, the local, are an outsider in your own neighbourhood … well then it kind of stops feeling like home. Plus there are a whole bunch of other factors that make living in that area more of a hassle than it is worth. Such as:

Tour buses. Of every size and shape, including huge buses barely able to navigate the narrow streets. These have been known to accidentally take a chunk out of people's houses, often historic buildings that jut right out to the edge of the sidewalk. Sometimes these mammoth vehicles become trapped, unable to move backwards or forwards in a narrow space. To combat this problem and appease the residents, the City of Reykjavík has now prohibited tour buses more than eight metres long in certain parts of the downtown area, restricting them to certain pick-up and drop-off points. Smaller buses, though, are still permitted, and these tend to hover around hotels both day and night, emitting smog and generally being noisy.

Suitcase wheels. The sound of those puppies on pavement at all hours is a major disturbance for many residents. Especially during the night when it interrupts their sleep.

Jacked-up prices. Shops and restaurants in "touristy" areas are more expensive than in other parts of the city, and people are fleeing the expense.

Walking tours. Imagine living downtown, maybe next to a little parkette, and every half hour from early in the morning until evening a walking tour stops there and the guide drones on for ten minutes. It might be all right the first time, but when you've heard the same spiel hundreds of times, or if you are trying to sleep in on the weekend, you might get a tad fed up.

Tourist shops. All the local businesses disappearing, and tourist shops that sell cheap trinkets opening up in their place. The Icelanders call them "puffin shops" because they all seem to sell stuffed puffins, which has become like the national bird of Iceland even though most Icelanders feel no special affiliation with it.

Parking. Finding a place to park in the downtown area is virtually impossible. Major annoyance.

Lack of community. Suddenly feeling like you're an outsider in your own community, because the "community" has become populated with people from all corners of the world who are just passing through, has driven many a local away.

The curious case of the missing Icelanders

So there is a mass exodus of Icelanders from the downtown area, and hard to find anyone wandering there who is not a tourist. But the strange thing is, even outside Reykjavík, tourists remark that they cannot find any Icelanders. They will tour the country for days, and the only natives they come across are those working in shops or restaurants—or maybe not even, since those jobs are increasingly being filled with migrant workers from abroad, who come to work in the service industry.

I became keenly aware of this separation between Icelanders and tourists a couple of years ago. Every spring, my husband and I drive around the country to drop off books and say hello to retailers. One of our favourite places on that route is the lovely and picturesque town of Seyðisfjörður, in the east. When we are there we book ourselves into the local hostel, not only because it is relatively inexpensive (yes, we Icelanders also feel the sting of the prices in our country) but also because it is exceptionally lovely.

Aside: I would recommend looking into the hostel option for anyone who wants to travel around Iceland without getting fleeced. They are not necessarily the youth hostels many of us are familiar with, where you sleep in a dorm filled with bunk beds with people you don't know. In many of them, including the hostel in Seyðisfjörður, you can book a private room, which will likely have its own sink, though you will have to share a toilet and shower. Also, sometimes you can arrange to have a made-up bed for a small fee.

Anyway, so there we are at the hostel in Seyðisfjörður. We head to the shared kitchen to prepare our dinner, and then to one of the tables in the dining area to eat. Before long we strike up a conversation with another couple at the table (as you do). We chat in English, and eventually ask them where they are from. "Switzerland," they answer, "and you?"

"From here. Iceland."

It takes them a second. I can see the wheels turning as they work to process the information. Then they break into a grin. "Icelanders!" they exclaim, "You are the first Icelanders we have had a conversation with since we arrived ten days ago!"

By this time, everyone in the room is staring at us. I can't help feeling a bit like a rare bird, spotted well outside its natural habitat.

In the time that has elapsed since then, I have repeatedly been asked where all the Icelanders are. One person added that, when she was in Iceland a few years ago, there were places downtown where the Icelanders consistently hung out. When she visited Iceland recently she went to those same places and saw no Icelanders at all—only tourists. Dismayed, she asked if we Icelanders had deserted all the places where we used to hang out.

I found the question intriguing, so with the help of Facebook I launched an informal survey among the Icelanders. Was it really the case that we were avoiding the places we had previously frequented, or had the tourist numbers simply reached such proportions that the locals had vanished in the sea of people?

I got a whole slew of responses. It was evident that people had opinions and wanted to share them. And to answer the original question, it would seem that, yes indeed, Icelanders have abandoned the places they used to go, especially—but not only—the ones in downtown Reykjavík. Here are some of the reasons they gave:

Prices. This was the primary reason folks had deserted their favourite hangouts: everything had shot up in price. In other words Icelanders keen to exploit tourists for profit are banishing their own countryfolk, and in the process robbing certain areas of the local flavour so appealing to those same tourists.

Too many tourists. This reason not only applied to downtown Reykjavík, but also places like the Laugardalslaug swimming pool, the largest outdoor pool in the city. It happens to be situated next to the main camping site and youth hostel in Reykjavík, and it is usually filled to the brim with foreign visitors. And although not expressly stated, I can pretty much guarantee that the Icelanders avoid this pool because they worry that people from abroad do not wash properly before going into the water. I think I speak for many Icelanders when I say that this is the first thing we think of when we encounter a foreigner at the pool.

Puffin shops. Icelanders have started avoiding downtown Reykjavík because they feel there are no shops for Icelanders any more. The downtown area has become filled with tourist shops (aka puffin shops) or ridiculously expensive design shops that ordinary Icelanders have no desire to shop in.

Can't speak their own language. With all those tourists coming in, service jobs in the tourism industry and beyond increasingly need to be filled by workers from abroad. The workers nearly all speak English, as do almost all Icelanders, but even so, it bothers the locals that they must speak a language not their own when they go out somewhere. People were also irked that so many signs and menus were in English.

Brief aside: discussions with people via social media have shown that non-Icelanders get even more indignant about this than Icelanders do. "Icelanders should not tolerate this!" they fume. "Employees should make people learn Icelandic before they give them a visa to work in Iceland!"

So why are the Icelanders more laid back about this than foreigners? Probably for a couple of reasons. One, Icelanders know how absurdly difficult the Icelandic language is to learn so they are willing to cut the non-natives some slack. Two, they are used to people coming in and working temporarily when the economy is booming. The Icelandic nation is tiny, and sometimes we just can't manage things on our own. And we know that the jobs that need to be filled simply cannot be filled if we insist that people learn to speak Icelandic first. Lately, though, it seems like maybe one in five service workers speaks Icelandic, and when you have to speak English *all the time* it can get a bit annoying. Not to mention worrying. After all, the Icelandic language is spoken by only a tiny proportion of people on a global scale, and there is always the concern that it may disappear completely.

As for making language proficiency a condition for a working visa … not doable. Iceland is a member of the European Economic Area, so anyone from any EEA member state can come to Iceland to work—the permit is simply a formality. Which means that if you are an EEA citizen and someone wants to give you a job in Iceland there is no way the government or any other administrative body can stop you from working, Icelandic proficiency or not.

The upside of this exodus of Icelanders from touristy areas is one that I don't believe anyone had foreseen: new life and vibrancy in neighbourhoods outside the downtown core. Cafés and restaurants that once were concentrated almost exclusively in the centre of Reykjavík are now springing up in various locations throughout the capital area, even in suburbs that previously were little more than bedroom communities. The tourist boom has thus led the Icelanders to create their own little pockets of life, away from the hordes and escalating prices. Which is a very good thing, making for livelier neighbourhoods and even helping to reduce carbon emissions.

A final word: even though the focus here is overwhelmingly on the negative aspects of the tourist invasion, by no means are all Icelanders displeased about the changes taking place in downtown Reykjavík. Many people welcome them wholeheartedly. These days there is far more happening downtown than before the tourism boom started, there are many more options for dining and socializing, and even more cultural activities than before.

Nothing is black and white. We may love one aspect of the change (all those new restaurants) and hate another (those higher prices). As I said before, it's complicated.

Tourists, any day

Take for instance a friend of mine, who would take tourists as neighbours over Icelanders any day. She lives in a downtown house that has three apartments, one of which is rented out as an Airbnb unit during the summer. In the winter, however … well, I'll let her tell it via a Facebook status she shared (published with her permission, and translated by yours truly, though it loses quite a bit in translation, sadly):

> ok (true story) :
>
> I have lived in 101 [postal code, downtown Reykjavík] for 13 years and in the last 6 years tourism has increased very rapidly and today there are lots of Airbnb rentals all around me. Many people (who live in the suburbs) think that tourists cause "a terrible disturbance" … but the truth is that tourists are a far better option than having Icelanders as neighbours … so much better, so much less disturbance, so much less noise, no parties, no hassle.
>
> Finally there is "calm" but also "life" in 101.
>
> Example: in the basement of the house where I live there is an Airbnb unit that is rented out all summer long. I hear nothing. No disturbance. No hassle. Despite the fact that hundreds of people from as many countries stay

> there. But then last winter the owner decided to rent the basement out to Icelanders...... jesus.
>
> That's when the fun really started—the father smoked and the smoke drifted into our bedroom. Whenever he went away to work for the weekend the son threw a party, with the same girls every time. Afterwards there were often (for some bizarre reason) used tampons in the garden and toilet paper...!!!??? (I never understood that) and sometimes the communal laundry room was left open... (great).
>
> We finally had peace again when the tourists came back :) that is when the hassle level dropped to 0.000000%
>
> The same goes for the camping trip that [daughter] and I just took: the tourists were = quiet, polite, neat and tidy.
>
> The Icelanders: kept us awake with barking dogs. They parked their cars next to our tent and turned on the ignition at 11 pm to heat them up... for 45 minutes! And of course they stashed garbage all over the place, which then blew away in the wind.

The rant concludes with a summary of the virtues of having tourists as neighbours, as opposed to Icelanders. No doubt this is often the case. After all, tourists generally come to a foreign country not to hang out in their rented digs, but to explore and sightsee. That means they usually leave the house in the morning, come back in the evening, and are in bed early so they can get the most out of the following day. As such, they're the perfect neighbours.

So as you can see, there is no standard answer to the question "how do the Icelanders feel about tourists". It totally depends on the circumstances, and the person.

Bad apple Adam

Just as there are some disrespectful and insensitive tourists around, there are some bad apples among the Icelanders. People who are more concerned with making a buck than ensuring top safety for their clients, or who have no problem screwing over their customers. Thankfully we do not often hear stories of that nature, but when we do it is always upsetting, as it reflects badly on the whole industry, and even the nation.

One particularly audacious story is that of the happily-now-defunct Hótel Adam (which the hotel's proprietors insisted on writing as Hotel AdaM and which I'll refrain from doing for aesthetic reasons … you're welcome) in downtown Reykjavík. It first caught the nation's attention when a sign on one of its walls appeared as a Facebook post by a concerned Icelander. The sign proclaimed, in capital letters: WE RECOMMEND DRINKING BOTTLED WATER[,]

NOT FROM THE TAP. (I inserted that comma there for clarity.) Conveniently, the Hotel Adam happened to sell some of that bottled water they recommended you drink, for the small fee of ISK 400 (USD 3) a pop.

Now, if you have ever been to Iceland you will probably know that to get fresh mineral water, fully compatible with anything out of a sealed bottle, you only have to turn on the nearest tap. The quality of Icelandic water is excellent. It is completely untreated with chemicals, and there is absolutely no reason not to drink it, unless there is something heinously wrong with your pipes.

The Icelander who posted the photo on Facebook therefore wondered whether something terrible had happened to the pipes on Skólavörðuholt, where Hotel Adam is located. A very logical question, for what other reason might there be to urge people not to drink out of the tap, and to pay good money for water?

And so, inspectors were promptly dispatched to the Adam to take stock of the water quality. On arriving there they found the owner absent (vacationing abroad) and staff working there who spoke no Icelandic. When asked who was in charge, a staff member furtively replied "no one". Their curiosity piqued, the inspectors decided to expand the scope of their investigation. They discovered that the Hotel Adam was operating rooms for which it had no licence, fire safety measures were hopelessly deficient, the food sold in the lobby had about as much nutritional value as a plastic bag, and was grossly overpriced to boot. It was further discovered that foreigners were working at the hotel without permits, and were being paid far below minimum wage. It was suggested that at least one employee was the victim of human trafficking. The hotel had not filed a tax return for the previous year, and the entire operation reeked of swindling and racketeering. Tests performed on the water came back a few days later, revealing not only that the tap water was perfectly fine to drink, but also that the bottled water sold at the hotel, the water they urged guests to buy, came from the hotel's own taps. BOOM.

As I mentioned, cases like these are extremely rare, but they do exist. A study by Icelandic magazine *Stundin* revealed that the exploitation of foreign workers in Iceland is real. Some foreigners working in tourism in Iceland are treated as virtual slaves. Cases like those often arise outside the capital area, in places where people are not easily able to associate with their peers, and are thus unprotected from the machinations of their employers.

All of which is to say, Klondike fever is rampant in certain parts of the Icelandic tourism industry, bringing out the worst in some people. So beware. Do some research, check reviews, avoid the scammers, and if you notice anything that looks like criminal activity—including human trafficking—please notify the police.

Heroes of the north

And now from the dark underbelly of Icelandic society, its swindlers and schemers, to its luminous side, those who selflessly risk their lives to help others. I am speaking of Iceland's Search and Rescue volunteers, whom we all love and revere.

Some countries have an emergency task force trained by the government to carry out various search and rescue missions. In some countries the task is entrusted to the military. In Iceland we have neither a governmental task force, nor a military. Instead we have the Icelandic Search and Rescue Association, which began as a citizens' initiative in 1928 and which still operates independently. Collectively known as ICE-SAR, it is made up of some 6,000 volunteers in 93 regional chapters around the country. Anyone who wishes to sign up to be an ICE-SAR volunteer has to undergo a rigorous training programme lasting 18 months, a portion of which they pay for out of their own pockets.

Whenever there is an emergency, like a missing person, an accident requiring a specialized response, or some other serious trouble, the regional team for that area is dispatched. In the event that a single team cannot cope, teams from other parts of the country are called out to assist. Those volunteers then do everything in their power to ensure that the situation is satisfactorily resolved, irrespective of how long it takes. The lengths to which the SAR teams have gone in order to ensure someone's safety or recover a body are astounding, from searching every inch of an area covering hundreds of square kilometres, to rappelling down into a glacier crevice that could close at any moment if there is a shift in the ice cap.

The amazing thing about ICE-SAR, apart from their professionalism and skill, is that they are entirely self-supporting. They receive no government funding. So in addition to conducting rescues, often in extremely hazardous situations, they are required to secure the funding that allows them to go out and perform those rescues. ICE-SAR primarily raises funds through the sale of fireworks around New Year's Eve, and the sale of key chains over a single weekend twice a year. Other than that, they rely on donations from the general public.

Here is what typically happens in an emergency: a call comes through and volunteers must drop everything to go out on a mission. They may be at work, in which case whatever they were doing must be put on hold, or their colleagues have to pick up the slack. Until now there has been a tacit agreement with employers that they let SAR volunteers leave work whenever needed, usually without deducting any pay. That is their contribution to this community effort. But if you are an employer, and your employee is suddenly taking an average of two out of five days a week off during the summer because he or she has to rescue people from situations that may be caused by their own recklessness or stupidity ... well, it goes without saying that generosity has its limits.

Then there is family. An ICE-SAR volunteer may have a spouse and children at home. Maybe this volunteer is due to pick up the kids from school or playschool while the spouse attends to other things. Suddenly everything is in upheaval because there is an emergency. Again.

No doubt it is wonderfully satisfying for an ICE-SAR volunteer to find a missing person alive, or to save someone from a potentially fatal situation. But imagine that you are called out, with all the inherent disruption, because someone has taken an impassable road in a Toyota Yaris when they were expressly told not to, or gone hiking on a glacier despite warnings and need to be rescued.

I am sure it can be pretty damn infuriating to donate large chunks of your life to something so senseless and preventable, especially when it happens repeatedly—which, unfortunately, it does.

The word on the street is that this cannot go on much longer, that SAR teams will have to start receiving some proper funding from the state, or start charging for rescue operations, particularly since the unbridled use of fireworks on New Year's Eve (primarily sold by ICE-SAR) has increasingly come under fire in recent years, for environmental reasons.

Yet the proposal to charge for rescues is a highly controversial one, and has always been rejected by ICE-SAR. Their argument is that a person in peril might think twice about calling for help if they were afraid they could not afford the rescue. If they waited, it might be too late. No doubt this concern is legitimate: the family I mentioned earlier in this book, who were found wandering in the fog with two small children on their way back from the volcanic eruption, initially refused help from ICE-SAR because they were afraid it would cost them too much.

And so, a couple of alternative ideas have been proposed. One is that travellers, especially people heading out on intrepid missions, should be made to buy insurance that would cover the cost of their rescue, if needed. Two, that the Icelandic government have the decency to fund ICE-SAR by allocating some of the tourist revenues for that purpose, in full or in part.

These are only ideas at the moment, and are not even close to being realized. Until they are, folks who need rescuing will have to continue relying on the goodwill of the local population, and the Icelanders' mad propensity for shooting up fireworks on New Year's Eve.

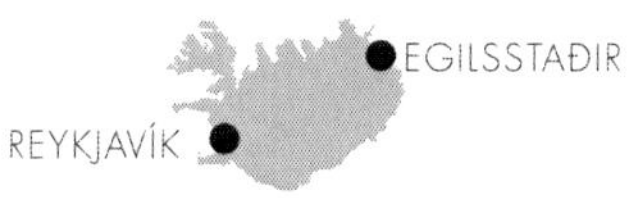

Bizarre tourist stories

Ever since the tourist boom started, we Icelanders regularly hear stories of what our visitors get up to. Some of them are mind-blowing, some hilarious, some mind-blowingly hilarious, and some quite appalling. Here are a few of the more colourful ones, in no particular order.

Rub a dub-dub at the car wash

Residents of Egilsstaðir in East Iceland were a tad taken aback one morning when they saw two men, completely naked, washing themselves in a self serve car wash. Such car washes are attached to every sizable petrol station in Iceland, and they are free of charge. The man who discovered the flagrant pair took it upon himself to educate them on the social mores of Iceland, which until now have not included the practice of showering naked at the car wash. This apparently annoyed one of the shower-happy gentlemen who promptly leapt up on a cement barrier and waved his pecker at the baffled instructor, yelling something at him in French. Which has me thinking that perhaps they were not tourists at all, but rather a particularly evolved (or not) strain of monkey.

Defecate in peace

So, we know about the toilet situation. We also know that when nature calls, there is little that can be done but to serve it. If you have read this far you should be well versed in the methodology of disposing of bodily wastes and associated paraphernalia (read: toilet paper) in Icelandic nature. You should also know enough to use your common sense as to where you do your business. Specifically: you do not want to be doing it on sacred ground. Like, say, at Þingvellir National Park, a place of immense historical and environmental significance, not only for Iceland, but for the world (Þingvellir is a UNESCO World Heritage Site). This is our sacred ground, our Westminster Abbey, the place where in the past we buried our statesmen and national heroes.

Those heroes rest in the churchyard in front of the pretty wooden church that you see on all the postcards from Þingvellir. It is in that churchyard, behind some bushes, that people have been defecating and leaving their toilet paper behind.

Even though there are public toilets just a few hundred metres away.

Now, you may legitimately ask: how do you know they are not Icelanders? We don't, of course, but I think we can pretty well rule it out. For one thing, this never happened before the tourist-slash-toilet thing became an issue. For another, there

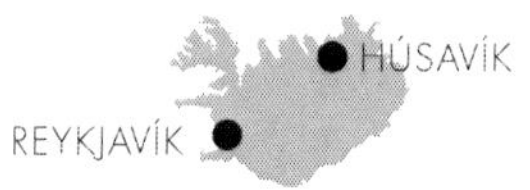

are not many Icelanders who would commit the sacrilege of shitting on the grave of Iceland's most revered national poet. That is a fact.

Just feeding the birds

Apropos the subject, an Icelandic woman in the town of Húsavík, in the north, came upon a female tourist who was having her children shit on the promenade next to the harbour—the very place where residents and tourists like to stroll. The local woman, completely aghast, asked the crafty mother what exactly she thought she was doing. The mother, who was busy wiping one of her children's butts at the time, went all furtive and retorted that there were no toilets anywhere so this had been an urgent necessity. The Icelandic woman informed her that there were toilets all over the vicinity, in every restaurant, museum, and café. At which the mother told her not to fret, since the birds would eat it anyway.

Strangely, no one in this part of the world has ever heard of the shit-eating birds of Húsavík—though of course I wouldn't presume to say that they don't exist.

Camp yard

A couple in Vík, south Iceland, arrived home from a short holiday abroad early one morning to find that someone had pitched a tent in their garden, beneath their living room window. At first they thought it might be someone they knew, who had turned up unannounced for a visit and hadn't found them at home. So they peered into the tent, only to see two large men "with very nice hats" sound asleep in their sleeping bags. "So I just closed the tent carefully," the woman, Helga Þorbergsdóttir, told the visir.is media site. The homeowners, being worn out from their trip, went to bed, and when they woke up later that day the tent and its occupants were gone. They were remarkably nonplussed about their nighttime visitors, adding that although people often park their camper vans behind their garage, they had never encountered anyone sleeping in their yard before. There is a first time for everything, I guess.

Holy snooze

Not everyone is as laid back about unwanted overnight guests, though. Residents of Reykhólar, on the southern West Fjords, were upset and angry when they discovered a Canadian pair had set up home in the town church and had even cooked a meal inside it on a portable gas stove that they had with them. The inside of the church is very obviously made of wood, and it does not take an Einstein to figure out how that escapade could have ended. Incidentally this was not the first time this had happened—a few months earlier locals had discovered a couple sleeping on the church pews. The impudent pair had taken the liberty of washing their clothes and spreading them out to dry all around them. Consequently the church at Reykhólar is now locked, something that was never done before.

Don't fall through the cracks

A group of tourists, with guide, touring on Langjökull glacier in a specially equipped vehicle, was stunned and amazed to discover a silver-coloured SUV up on the ice cap, quite a distance from civilization. The occupants were a couple with three small children, including one toddler, who were traipsing around on the ice cap, having a boo at the scenery. Let me repeat, in case it didn't register: *a couple with three small children, including one toddler, traipsing around on the ice cap*. The Icelandic tour guide stopped the vehicle, rolled down his window, and asked the couple what they thought they were doing. "Am I doing something wrong?" asked the bewildered father-slash-intrepid glacial explorer. The tour guide attempted to explain to him that it wasn't a great idea to take your family onto a glacier that was ever-shifting and unpredictable, filled with deadly cracks and holes, in a vehicle not equipped for driving on ice.

I guess the moral of the story, apart from the Darwinian angle, is that we Icelanders cannot assume, as we have for so many years, that all our guests are aware of the dangers of travelling in Iceland. Which probably means that signs proclaiming DO NOT GO ON A SUICIDE MISSION UP ON THIS GLACIER or similar are in our future, for better or worse.

Naked boy on a ledge

Arguably the most heart-wrenching tourist story is the one of the naked child stuck on a ledge. The setting is Þingvellir National Park, where two tectonic plates are pulling apart at a rate of a few centimetres per year. This geological phenomena results in a great number of gorges and ravines, many of which are filled with pure spring water and are popular sites for snorkelling and diving. This spring water of which I speak is freezing cold—around 2 degrees Celsius (35 Fahrenheit) year-round, which is even colder than the sea around Iceland.

Temperatures like that can easily make your muscles seize up within minutes, making swimming impossible and drowning inevitable.

At any rate, an Icelandic park employee came upon a family who had dared their teenage son to hop naked into the ravine. The son had accepted the dare, jumped in, and immediately discovered that he was severely out of his depth in more ways than one. Luckily he managed to swim a couple of strokes over to the rugged cliff wall, then to scramble onto a ledge where he lay, in physical shock, while his family had a good old laugh at his expense. (I am going to be extremely generous here and presume they were not aware of the danger to which he had been subjected.) The boy's brother helped him clamber to safety as the park employee gave the family a piece of his mind, warning them on parting not to roast any marshmallows in the volcanic eruption that was going on at the time.

Noel, Noel

And then there is the story of the affable Noel.

Noel was an American tourist who came on his first visit to Iceland in February 2016. He rented a car at Keflavík airport and set off for the Hótel Frón on Laugavegur in Reykjavík, about an hour's drive from the airport, where he had booked a room. However, when he typed the hotel's address into his GPS device he mistakenly added an extra "r" in Laugavegur, so it became "LaugaRvegur". It just so happens that Laugarvegur is a legitimate Icelandic street name, but the only place in Iceland where there is a Laugarvegur is in the small town of Siglufjörður, in the north.

So Noel sets off driving, and finds it a bit odd that his GPS is not following the signs for Reykjavík. Assuming that his technology knows Iceland better than he does, he drives and drives, enjoying the beautiful scenery. After a while, though, he starts to get a tad anxious since the roads are icy and he's driving a small compact car. Also, he had read somewhere that he should stick to south Iceland since the north was far more risky in terms of weather … yet here he is, most definitely travelling north. Twice he stops to punch in the address, and each time it points him in the same direction.

Five hours later, Noel arrives on Laugarvegur in Siglufjörður. Holding a stub of paper in his hand with his presumed address on it, he knocks on the door and asks the woman who opens if he is in the right place. "I thought he was joking," the woman, Sigurlína Káradóttir, told visir.is. She explained to him that he was, indeed, on Laugarvegur, but not in Reykjavík. To which Noel responded: "Is it far?"

So Sigurlína calls Hótel Frón to inform them that Noel will not be arriving that day as planned. Instead he checks into the

Hótel Siglufjörður for the night. The following morning he wakes to find that his hapless escapade is all over the news and he is now famous in Iceland. He is such a celebrity, in fact, that the hotel owners invite him to stay another night, completely free of charge, which he happily accepts.

Two days later Noel finally arrives at the Hótel Frón in Reykjavík. At this point it has been discovered that Hótel Frón's address is, in fact, written with an extra "r" on a couple of large online booking sites. Noel, therefore, is vindicated of any stupidity in this little comedy of errors. At the Frón, meanwhile, he receives a royal welcome, is upgraded from a regular single room to a deluxe suite, and invited down to their restaurant for a complimentary dinner and drinks. Soon the operators of the Blue Lagoon, Iceland's most popular tourist spot, are on the phone, asking Noel if he would care to visit them, free of charge. As if that is not enough, every media outlet wants to interview him, folks are stopping him on the street asking to take selfies with him, and the BBC even reports on his cross-country adventure on their website.

And all because of a single misplaced "r".

Soon after Noel leaves Iceland, Hótel Siglufjörður rolls out a new TV commercial. And who is the star? Who else but the endearing Mr. Noel.

THE TRUTH ABOUT THOSE ICELAND MYTHS

True or false?

Since we are nearing the end of this little book, I thought we might wrap things up with a little game of True and False.

To put it another way: how about we examine some of the more common myths about Iceland? You know, the ones that get shared on memes all over Internetland until they take on a life of their own and it becomes impossible to tell people what really happened because they "saw it on the Internet!" and the things they saw were the things they wanted to believe. Myths like the following:

There are no trees in Iceland

False. They may not be very large or very numerous, but there are definitely trees.

Once upon a time, apparently, Iceland was covered in forest. But when the first settlers came they cut down all the trees for firewood, in part because they liked taking saunas (no joke). Their sauna room was the *baðstofa*—literally "bath lounge". But alas, two things happened. One, all the trees were cut down and, given the arctic climate, they were not able to grow back fast enough. Two, the Little Ice Age came, and since by this time the Icelanders had used up all their forests they were kinda in a tough spot. Gradually, over time, their houses were made smaller to conserve heat, and people gravitated into the room where the fire was kept burning, which was the baðstofa. Of course by then they had long stopped taking saunas, but the name stuck. For the next few centuries, the Icelanders lived in that little baðstofa—literally. It was the room where everyone slept, ate, worked, and generally lived out their earthly existence.

Iceland has managed to grow back some of its forests through concerted efforts at planting trees. Given the climate, though, those trees grow slowly, and are not large, at least by international standards. Most of the forests are birch forests, and birch trees are rarely tall. Hence this common joke, known to every Icelander:

Q: What do you do when you are lost in an Icelandic forest?

A: Stand up.

Icelanders believe in elves

Elves are very much a part of the Icelanders' daily lives. For instance, Icelanders never build anything unless they get permission from the elves first, because the building site may be an elf colony, and if it is all their equipment explodes.

For some odd reason, the foreign media adores this myth. They love to present Icelanders as a bunch of endearing kooks who believe in elves, which they sometimes call fairies (as though elves and fairies are the same thing, which they are not). When I point out that, while this belief was widely held among our ancestors in the old days, there are few people who subscribe to it now, they metaphorically pat my head and say something like: "It's all right, you don't need to be ashamed, that's no weirder than believing that a man with a white beard lives up in the sky". Or they get a bit tetchy and announce that they know for a fact that Icelanders believe in elves because they read about a study at the University of Iceland that said something like 90 percent of Icelanders believe in elves, and also it said so in a video on the Icelandair in-flight entertainment system so it must be true.

Trying to set the record straight on this one is like repeatedly beating your head against a basalt column. The truth is irrelevant because no matter how often you tell it, no one seems to hear it. But I'll say it anyway: the majority of people in Iceland do not believe in the existence of elves. They do not speak to elves. They do not think about elves on a daily basis. And they most certainly wouldn't not build their house somewhere because the elves might disapprove.

Not that we don't recognize elves or hidden people (two terms that mean the same thing) as part of our cultural heritage. We do, and are very much aware that most of our ancestors believed in them. Incidentally, those mythical beings had very little in common with the diminutive folks in green with the pointy ears—the image that probably springs to most people's minds when they hear the word "elves". They were tall, regal beings that inhabited a hidden world parallel to our own. Many tales of these hidden people exist, and scholars today believe that stories of them helped Icelanders in the old days cope with the overwhelming harshness of their lives. For instance, stories of hidden people who abducted children and raised them as their own were probably the parents' way of processing the grief of a child that had gone missing, which in centuries past happened as a matter of course.

As for not building anything without talking to the elves first—this is also baloney. Granted, there have been documented instances where people halted construction projects because their equipment broke down or things went consistently wrong. They believed the hidden people were sending them a message, requesting that they would stop building on their land. In one instance a road was diverted around a boulder that folks had in the past believed to be the habitat of the elves. So yes, this has happened. But it is not commonplace, nor routine. These are isolated instances, that happened decades or centuries ago, and those people who complied with the elves' alleged wishes are hardly representative of the entire Icelandic nation—not by a long shot.

There was an article several years ago in *Vanity Fair*, penned by celebrated author Michael Lewis. He had come to Iceland following the economic meltdown and was supposedly reporting from the trenches. The article was filled with claims that ranged from dubious to outright false, among them that Icelanders were blowing up their Range Rovers on the street for insurance money (completely false). Also, that the construction of a large Alcoa aluminium smelter in East Iceland had only been given the go-ahead after the elves who lived on the building site had been consulted.

It sounded suitably weird and Lewis had no qualms about including it in his article. The only problem being that it was untrue. Here is what really happened: when a large-scale construction project is launched in Iceland, archaeological mapping is done to determine whether the building site is one of historical significance. For instance if there were any known battles on the site, if it was used as a graveyard, if the site is mentioned in the Icelandic Sagas, or if there are any folk stories or legends associated with it. Those folk stories or legends may or may not involve elves. They may also involve trolls, or outlaws, or ghosts. Whatever. These sorts of findings are simply recorded, and if it is determined that there may be artifacts on the site, some excavation work is usually done.

This archaeological mapping, in the spin put on by *Vanity Fair*, suddenly became "asking the elves for permission". And alas, *Vanity Fair* has a far larger audience than a few Icelandic voices shouting in the desert, so correcting this little "alternative fact" became an impossibility. From there the idea snowballed, other foreign media outlets took it and ran with it, and a myth was born. Some Icelanders, primarily those connected with tourism, saw an opportunity for profit, so they jumped on the bandwagon, creating elf tours, an elf school, and all sorts of elf-related paraphernalia.

So if you want to take a course at the elf academy or tour the elf colonies, by all means do, but be aware that there are two sides to every story, and don't swallow the propaganda whole.

Iceland is completely dark in the winter and light in the summer

Some folks think that, at some point in the fall, the sun in Iceland sets and does not rise again until the following spring. In other words, that there is full and complete darkness for several months of the year. "How can you cope with the winters?" they ask, genuinely concerned.

But it is not like that.

Yes, Iceland has more darkness in the winter than in the summer, but it doesn't go from one day being light all the time, to the next being dark all the time. It happens gradually. Following the summer solstice on June 21 the days slowly start to get shorter, with sunrise and sunset times closer together each day until there are only about three and a half hours of daylight between them—even less in the north.

That doesn't mean, though, that it is dark the rest of the time. Even though the sun does not rise in the early morning, it is there hovering below the horizon, and sending light. So we get these long extended sunrises, and long extended sunsets. It may start to get light around 9 am and then you will get this full spectrum of a sunrise happening slowly over the next two and a half hours. Then we'll have normal daylight for three and a half hours, after which the process begins again, only in reverse: the sun setting very slowly, with this drawn-out sunset, replete with a symphony of colour—red and gold and mauve and pink and blue and purple.

This, of course, is assuming that it's not cloudy. If it's cloudy you'll get about 50 shades of grey.

So, contrary to what many people think, winter in Iceland is actually a time of amazing colours in the sky: sunrises, sunsets, and the spectacular northern lights, with all their undulating nuances and shades.

Icelandic women are really easy to get into bed

You just need to go to a bar and soon a long-legged, blonde woman will make bedroom eyes at you and soon thereafter go with you to your hotel room where she will have hot steamy sex with you all night. And if you want her to, she'll bring a friend.

OK, you with the juvenile schoolboy fantasy, I hate to burst your bubble, but here is the thing. Icelandic women generally have more important (and interesting) things on their minds than hopping into the sack with any old (or young) dude that crosses their path. Also? They have standards. So if your main purpose in visiting Iceland is to get yourself seduced by a hot blonde, then take my advice and stay home. Save yourself some dosh.

(You're welcome.)

On that note, though … Icelandic people, men *and* women, tend to have fewer sexual hangups than people in many other parts of the world. Maybe because being naked is not that taboo in Iceland, a happy byproduct of showering naked at the pool. Icelandic women are emancipated, so as a rule they're not uncomfortable picking and choosing if, when, or with whom they want to have sex. Does this mean they'll have sex with anyone? Hell, no. It just means they're not hung up about having it when they want to have it. And be most assured: Icelandic women do not go out to bars because they want to find someone with whom to have sex. They go out to have fun with their friends, dance, socialize and have a laugh. Sure, maybe they'll meet someone in a bar that they'll connect with, be attracted to, and maybe go home with. Or not. It's up to them.

Icelanders eat really disgusting food

Putrid shark. Sheeps' heads. Ram's testicles. Whale meat. These are basically the national dishes of Iceland, and Icelanders eat them all the time.

Um, no. Icelanders rarely eat those foods. They like to make tourists eat them, though, and laugh uncontrollably when they grimace and cough and look like they're about to vomit. So be forewarned.

Yet those foods do exist, and here is why. Iceland used to be really poor. A century ago it was the poorest country in Europe. In those days, food was really scarce, and everything that could possibly be eaten was eaten. This meant that every part of the sheep was either consumed, or used. I say "sheep" because Icelanders generally did not eat other animals. They were far too valuable for the other services they provided—the cow (there was usually only one, if that) for producing milk, the horses for transport, dogs for herding and companionship, and so on.

So the wool of the sheep was used for clothes and blankets, the skin for shoes and outer layers, the meat and offal for food, the bones as toys for children.

Sure, you may be thinking, I get that, but why was the food so disgusting? Well, because back in those days, preserving food was a real challenge. Our ancestors couldn't just toss stuff into the freezer like we do today. They had to do things like pickle stuff, or dry stuff, or salt stuff (although even salting was problematic, since salt as a commodity was in short supply). That's why we have, for example, pickled whale blubber, pickled ram's testicles, and dried fish.

The infamous cured shark (often referred to as "rotten shark", "putrid shark" or "peed-on shark") that tourists sometimes try at their peril, is a chapter unto itself. This, ahem, *delicacy* developed because the species known as Greenland shark was caught by fishermen and, of course, eaten. The only problem was that the meat of the Greenland shark is highly toxic due to its high urea and trimethylamine oxide content, so if you ate it untreated you would die. Consequently it was buried in the ground, on a bed of gravel, and heavy stones were put on top to press out the fluids. After lying that way for a few weeks, the shark was removed and hung out to dry for several months, after which time it was ready to be eaten. By this time it was no longer toxic, but still had a very, shall we say, *pungent* flavour.

Nowadays, the only time most of this food gets hauled out is when the Icelanders want to punk tourists, or at special festivals called Þorrablót, held in late January or early February. Those festivals are a throwback to the past, and have to do with the pagan festivals that were held in secret after Christianity was made the official religion and paganism was outlawed. Apart from that, we rarely see the stuff.

So no, our food is not at all horrible. In fact, you'll likely discover that Icelandic food is pretty damn excellent. The truth—and I say this with all modesty—is that it is pretty difficult to find a bad meal in Iceland. You have to try extra hard. The culinary standards at restaurants are high, the fish is fresh, the lamb is amazing, the dairy products yummy. We eat well.

So if some local tells you that you have to try the putrid shark because it is a local delicacy, you can call them out and tell them that you know better. Then go ahead and try it. I would. (No really, I would.)

Iceland had a revolution and crowdsourced a new constitution, written for and by the people

Yes, well, we had a revolution of sorts after the country's economy tanked in 2008, and the shocking mismanagement and corruption of our elected leaders and top businesspeople were exposed for all to see. Folks took to the streets to protest, slowly at first, then building in momentum, until one of the coalition parties resigned so that the government effectively collapsed.

We had elections, and got a new government. Then in November 2009 a group of grassroots organizations decided to call a National Assembly, where people mostly chosen randomly from the national registry were invited to participate. The meeting was in session for a full day and when it was finished presented a set of values that its participants hoped would serve as guiding principles for the reconstruction of Icelandic society, and the direction they wanted the nation to take. Number one was integrity, then honesty, equal rights, respect, justice and so on.

This work, along with that of a second, government-run 2010 National Assembly, was used as the basis for writing a new constitution for the nation. A constitutional draft was drawn up by a group of 25 democratically elected representatives. There were some snags along the way in getting the process set up (more on all that online if you are interested, simply search for "Icelandic constitutional reform"), that affected the authority of the council. However, in the end they got to work and for five months debated various issues openly and transparently, and posted them online, where the public was also invited to have its say. The final draft was presented in July 2010, but required parliamentary approval. Many of the articles in the draft were contentious, including ownership of natural resources and electoral reforms. The government was not able to get the draft passed before elections, and the subsequent government of the Progressive and Independent Parties effectively stuck the constitutional draft into a drawer, where it has remained ever since.

So yes—almost all true, right up until the point where the constitution needed approval. It has been stuck at that stage since then because the parties in power are not keen on some of the proposed amendments that will most certainly diminish their power and that of their cronies to exploit the country's resources for their own gain. No doubt it will stay that way until a government is elected that is less concerned with special interests and more with the common good. When that will be, is anyone's guess.

Iceland has an app to prevent relatives from sleeping with each other, called the "incest app"

Before I even address this question, imagine that you live in a country with a population of approximately 360,000 people. Of those, around 228,000 live in the largest urban centre. Consider also that family ties in that country tend to be very close, and extended families meet up at weddings, christenings, confirmation parties, funerals, and a multitude of other events.

What I'm getting at? Basically that if you were so closely related to someone that sleeping with them would constitute incest, *you wouldn't need a damn app to tell you.* You would have met up with them a million times already in your life.

That said, where there is smoke there is fire, and this stupid story about the incest app does have a basis in reality. You see, there is a company in Iceland called DeCode Genetics, that studies and researches Icelanders' DNA. Back in its early days, DeCode created a website called Íslendingabók (The Book of Icelanders). This website, still going strong, is effectively a genealogy database that allows you to trace your lineage, see how you are related to someone, and pull up all sorts of info about your ancestors, including where they lived, what they did, who they married, who were their children, when they died, and more.

It truly is an excellent and fascinating resource, and there are likely few places in the world where such a thing would be possible. In Iceland, however, due to the small and relatively isolated population (at least up until the 20th century), it is fairly easy to map these things out. All Icelanders, it turns out, are related at least eight generations back, and most people less than that.

So naturally when smartphones started taking over the world, it made sense for the Íslendingabók website to be made into an app. So now we Icelanders can do the same thing that we have been doing for over a decade online—checking out our lineage, but on our phones. Meanwhile some foreign media outlets picked up on this and turned it into a whoo-whoo story about Icelanders being in a bar and looking at their app to see if they were about to sleep with their relative.

Which is just absurd.

Iceland is going to power the UK and rest of Europe with green energy

The scary thing about this crazy myth is that so many high-profile people actually believe that it is a possibility and go around talking about it.

As you may know by now, Iceland gets its energy largely from hydroelectric and geothermal sources. Someone got the idea that if you laid a sub-oceanic cable from Iceland to the UK, the UK and Europe could tap into Iceland's "green" energy (open to debate … geothermal energy harnessing also has a pretty serious environmental impact, as I alluded to before) and everything would be hunky dory. Fewer CO^2 emissions, less greenhouse effect, all that wonderful stuff.

Only, this is just so poorly thought out. Because for Iceland to be able to power even a medium sized city in the UK, you would need to harness practically every waterfall, brook, hot spring, geyser, river and streamlet in Iceland. The power plants we have already barely manage to supply our domestic needs, to say nothing of the needs of an entire freaking continent.

The only thing that makes sense in this crazy idea is if surplus power that is currently wasted—power that is being generated but not used, for example during the night—was sent through the cable to be sold elsewhere. But even so, it would only be a tiny percentage of what is required, and might be able to power, say, Croydon. For a night.

So—no. I don't see Iceland's volcanoes powering the UK or any part of Europe. At least I hope that no one would be stupid enough to sacrifice the entirety of our beautiful landscapes for such an end. After all, our foreign visitors do not come to Iceland to look at power plants. They come for the pristine, unspoiled landscapes, and those need our protection.

Iceland has no crime and no army

As I wrote about on page 40, Iceland is relatively safe—"relatively" being the operative word. I say that because the number of murders committed in Iceland is actually higher than many people think. From 2001-2020 there were 36 homicides in Iceland, which works out to just under two a year. But crime is not just murder, and Iceland has plenty of the other kind: theft, break-ins, assaults, rape, drug-related crimes, and so on. Violent crime, thankfully, is not something you see or hear of every day, but that doesn't mean it never happens.

As for Iceland having no army, this is essentially true. There are no Icelandic armed forces ... after all, with such a minuscule population it would be a bit of a tough call. Instead Iceland is in a defence partnership, as a member of NATO. It offers a strategic location for the NATO partners to set up camp, which is why the U.S. Air Force had a base in Iceland from the end of WWII until 2005, when the Cold War had thawed and the US pulled its forces out of the country. Recently, what with tensions mounting between Russia and the West, there has been talk of the US returning to its former base in Keflavík, but as yet this has not happened, though a rather nebulous "increased collaboration" was announced in 2016.

So even though the Icelandic people do not don military gear and go out to fight wars, they are party to a military force that does, namely NATO. As such, Iceland was on the list of nations in the "coalition of the willing" during the Iraq invasion, and effectively supports any military operations in which NATO is involved. So you could say, yes, that Iceland has no army—and yet it is a nation that participates in military activities, in conjunction with its allies.

And finally, the mother of all myths, the one that has spawned countless internet memes and refuses to die no matter how often you cut off its head:

Iceland jailed the corrupt bankers and politicians, refused to bail out the banks, and forgave everyone's debts

OK, let's break this one down into its components, shall we?

Iceland jailed the bankers. Well, yes and no. After the banks melted down and the country was on the edge of national bankruptcy, it seemed likely (understatement) that some illicit activity had taken place. As a result, the Icelandic government created a special prosecutor's office, prosaically dubbed The Special Prosecutor's Office, that was charged with investigating economic crimes. These investigations took a very, very long time—so long that the Special Prosecutor-haters got lots of food for their vitriol and even the most pro-SPO among us were starting to get fidgety. At long last, *years* later, a few indictments were made, most of which resulted in acquittals. As we knew they probably would: economic crime is notoriously difficult to investigate and prove, plus the defendants had plenty of dosh to hire the best lawyers. Eventually, though, some of those indictments did end in convictions and a handful of high-ranking executives received relatively long sentences. So, there is a kernel of truth in the first part of that myth, but it was miles from being *all* the bankers.

And those who were convicted? Lest you imagine they were tossed into the maximum-security slammer with the rest of the riff-raff, think again. They got the best possible treatment, meaning a stint in the open (no fences) white-collar prison on Snæfellsnes, known as Kvíabryggja. There they had access to computers, cellphones and the Internet. Oh, and a golf course. Plus they got regular outings to a nearby town to buy ice cream with their prison guard. But it was not all fun and games: an attempt to organize a horse riding excursion was thwarted when prison authorities refused to buy the justification that it was a "training course" designed to improve the inmates' competence for tackling life outside the slammer. Prison authorities also nixed the bankers' bid to have their own private chauffeurs pick them up and drive them into Reykjavík so they could attend trials—which the inmates in question protested loudly in the media via their own personal PR representatives.

The longest sentences, given to four executives from Kaupthing bank, were four to six years. But a year into their sentences the Icelandic parliament deftly passed a law that allowed for shorter sentence terms, and the four were promptly released from Kvíabryggja. *Wot?*—Such was the prevailing sentiment among the Icelanders, too. Could it possibly be that said law had been specially written for those four white-collar criminals, who still held sway in Icelandic society? Naturally the suggestion was vehemently denied by all camps—yet it seemed a tad too happy a coincidence not to have been engineered.

But wait—it gets better. So our fabulous four were released from Kvíabryggja prison and sent to a halfway house in Reykjavík where they were supposed to serve the remaining few months of their (shortened) sentence. They were free to go about their business during the day and evening, with the stipulation that they had to return for dinner, and be back for bed at 11 pm.

Then, in May 2016, a helicopter crashed in the Hengill area, about an hour's drive east of Reykjavík. Further investigation revealed that on board was one of our favoured convicts, entertaining overseas business associates in his own personal chopper. The Icelandic nation was outraged. Here was this individual, a resident of a halfway house funded by taxpayers, "paying his debt to society", yet having a grand old time hosting clients on sightseeing flights during the day. Sure, he was not technically breaking any rules, but was this morally and ethically sound? Was justice being served? Was there rehabilitation involved? Was the system doing what it was supposed to do? Are those Internet memes correct? You decide.

Iceland jailed corrupt politicians. Wrong. Here is what happened: there was an indictment of one Geir H. Haarde, who was prime minister of Iceland prior to and during the economic meltdown. He was charged with gross negligence in the line of duty plus a couple of other minor offenses, by a special court that was established in 1905 to hold trials over government ministers. Haarde was acquitted of all charges, except a rather inane one of failing to hold cabinet meetings in the lead-up to the meltdown. For that he received a suspended sentence. One of the main criticisms of the trial was that the court in question had never before convened, it was seen as completely outdated, and the trial itself was viewed by some as a vehicle for exacting revenge by a bloodthirsty, angry mob. So no, Geir Haarde, Iceland's "corrupt politician", was not jailed. In fact, he was later made Iceland's Ambassador to the United States with a seat in Washington DC—likely the most coveted ambassadorial post there is in this country. He then moved on to take a seat on the Board of the World Bank, as representative for the Nordic and Baltic states, serving there from 2019-2021.

Iceland refused to bail out the banks. Makes it sound a lot nobler than it actually was. The truth: Iceland couldn't afford to bail out the banks. By the time the economy melted down, Iceland's three commercial banks had grown to 11 times the country's GDP. Icelandic authorities were forced to let them go bankrupt because it was either that or national bankruptcy on a colossal scale.

Iceland forgave everyone's debts. It is a tad difficult to say exactly how this myth was born, but here are a couple of theories.

1. When the Icelandic economy melted down, lots of people had car loans and mortgages that were denominated in foreign currencies. The reason for why this was is complex, but the important thing to note is that people owed money in currencies other than Icelandic króna. When the banks collapsed, the value of the króna plummeted. So people suddenly owed double, or triple, or quadruple what they had owed at the beginning, since they were making payments in a currency that had sharply devalued against the currency in which their loan was made. People were really, seriously struggling, and some just gave up and declared bankruptcy. After about two years of this, the Icelandic Supreme Court ruled that it had been illegal for the banks to issue loans in foreign currencies. The loans were recalculated as though they had initially been issued in Icelandic krónur, and the banks themselves had to take the hit for the discrepancy in value between the two currencies. So in that sense, people who had been in serious debt were suddenly offered debt relief—but only because it was determined that they had been duped previously, and their loans were recalculated to reflect the original amount, only in krónur.

2. Another potential scenario concerns mortgage debt. Most people in Iceland had, and still have, mortgages in good old Icelandic krónur. Now, almost all loans and mortgages are indexed to the rate of inflation. This means that, as inflation goes up, the principal of your loan also goes up, so your mortgage just keeps getting bigger and bigger along with the rate of inflation, even if you are making regular monthly payments. Compounding the problem for many people was that, in the three-or-so years before the meltdown, a real estate bubble had formed. This meant that all the people who had bought properties during that period, especially those who were buying their first property (read: young people starting out in life), had taken out large mortgages, and were already struggling to make the payments. It stands to reason that when you are already having a hard time meeting your payments and suddenly have to pay 50 percent more, it's a financial deathblow.

So people were going bankrupt and losing their homes left and right—a bad, bad scenario. Then in 2013 we had national elections, and one of the parties in the running, the Progressive Party (a complete misnomer), promised debt relief to everyone whose mortgage had increased so sharply. When questioned as to how they planned to finance this massive debt-relief package, the then-leader of the PP, Sigmundur Davíð Gunnlaugsson (he of the infamous Panama Papers scandal, who was forced to resign as PM after he was caught lying on TV) replied that he had a stellar plan. He would tax the hedge funds who still had Icelandic krónur trapped inside the country. This was a result of capital control measures being implemented when the banks collapsed, which shut down all transport of funds out of Iceland (long and complicated story). The PP estimated the debt relief package would cost around ISK 300 billion (around USD 2.1 billion), which would all be taken from the bad foreigners (the PP, at least at the time, were notoriously xenophobic and populist) whose money was in lockdown inside the steel walls of the Icelandic economy.

Long story short—the PP was elected, and here is what they did: first, they abolished taxes on the rich, including their closest associates and friends. Then they raised taxes on basic necessities like food. Then, they basically kicked back and chilled. Months passed, and folks kept asking "Where is my debt relief at?" But no answers came. Until, finally, when the natives were starting to get super restless, a big old press conference was called where, to great fanfare, the debt relief package was announced: ISK 80 billion (USD 560 million) would be allocated to help those poor unfortunates who had been victims of the systemic collapse (not ISK 300 billion, as reported previously) and it would be taken from the state treasury—not from the bad old foreigners who, it turned out, had never even been consulted.

It has later been made public that those who received the highest amount of this "debt relief" were the richest one percent in Iceland. Meanwhile, everyone paid for it, including those who owned no properties and therefore got no debt relief, who were maybe on the rental market and were being run into the ground financially by astronomical rents. In short, the debt relief package was a big old sham.

Meanwhile the politicians slapped each other on the back with self-congratulatory glee and made sure to turn this complete atrocity into a splendid success with all the Orwellian tactics at their disposal.

But wait—we have an epilogue. The real clincher came in April 2016, when Sigmundur Davíð Gunnlaugsson sat down to speak to a journalist from the Swedish national broadcaster SVT. The latter, after a few harmless questions, suddenly blindsides Sigmundur Davíð Gunnlaugsson with an enquiry about an offshore company named Wintris. The PM, after an initial moment of pure, excruciating shock, makes little of his affiliation with Wintris, until the reporter pulls out a document bearing his signature and proving his ties to Wintris—leaked, of course, via the Panama Papers. The interview was widely circulated internationally, and the PM was forced to resign a few days later after being publicly humiliated.

Now, the point in that story that many folks outside of Iceland miss is that Wintris, with its hidden ownership, had claims in the bankrupt Icelandic banks, and money locked inside Iceland. In fact, Wintris was one of those "bad foreigners" that the PP had promised to tax, in order to pay for the debt relief package. In other words, the PM had secretly been promising to tax himself … probably knowing all the time that he wouldn't do it because his own interests weighed stronger than the national interests. And, of course, in the end he didn't.

Yet these sorts of complexities do not lend themselves well to Internet memes that claim that Iceland forgave everyone's debts.

So there we have it. The most common misconceptions about Iceland and the Icelandic people, laid bare. And, I hope, something to help right the scales of truth.

IN CLOSING

As I pointed out at the beginning of this book, this treatise on the state of Icelandic tourism anno 2023 is far from comprehensive. For that I would need a lot more space, infinitely more research, and by the time such a book were finished, everything would probably already have changed. Instead I have touched upon the more prominent facets of the industry, given a few examples by way of elaboration, and hopefully entertained a bit along the way. Ultimately, though, I hope that these pages have managed to provide some perspective, and that we locals and our esteemed visitors have been brought slightly closer in our understanding of one another.

If you have enjoyed this little gander at the current state of Iceland's tourism industry and think it might be useful for others to read, I would be very grateful if you could recommend it to your friends. Also, a review and rating on Amazon would be very much appreciated. Ratings are extremely important for authors and publishers, as it helps others who may be interested to find the book in question.

Thank you for reading, and happy responsible touring—in Iceland, or wherever your travels take you.

USEFUL WEBSITES AND APPS

en.vedur.is - the latest weather updates
road.is - the most recent road conditions
safetravel.is - all about touring safely
visiticeland.com - official tourism website for Iceland
visitreykjavik.com - official tourism website for Reykjavík
campinginiceland.com - all campsites in Iceland
museumguide.is - a guide to all Icelandic museums
whatson.is - events calendar
icelandreview.com - news and reviews
restaurants.is - a listing of all restaurants
appyhour - a phone app with info about happy hour deals
map.is - excellent map of Iceland
bus.is - for bus lines in Reykjavík and beyond
icelandwithkids.is - the name says it all
Travel Iceland Facebook group
Iceland Q&A Facebook group
Facebook.com/AldaSigmundsdottir - 'nuff said

ACKNOWLEDGEMENTS

I am very grateful to all the people who helped with the writing and production of this book. To my beta readers Brian Butler, Erin Dowling-Kane, Kathleen Gudmundsson, Stephen Cowdery and Vida Morkunas—thank you for your invaluable feedback and suggestions that helped to make this book so much better than it otherwise would have been. To Megan Herbert, whose illustrations lift the text to a higher level and who is always such a joy to work with. And to Erlingur Páll Ingvarsson, for being my partner in crime, books, life, and everything else. Many thanks also to the people who subscribe to my newsletter and who sent me the questions they had concerning Iceland and tourism. They really helped me understand the areas that people wanted to know more about, and as such laid the foundation for this book.

ABOUT THE AUTHOR

Alda Sigmundsdóttir is a writer, journalist and translator, and the author of seven other books about Iceland. She has written extensively about Iceland for the international media and is a frequent commentator on Icelandic affairs. Catch up with Alda on her website aldasigmunds.com, where you can also sign up for her newsletter. You can find Alda on Facebook, Twitter and Instagram.

Other books by Alda Sigmundsdóttir, available through Amazon or on aldasigmunds.com:

Daughter - a Memoir

The Little Book of Icelandic

The Little Book of the Icelanders

The Little Book of the Icelanders in the Old Days

The Little Book of the Hidden People

The Little Book of the Icelanders at Christmas

Icelandic Folk Legends

The Little Book of Days in Iceland - An any-year planner

Unraveled - a Novel About a Meltdown

Living Inside the Meltdown

The following is an excerpt from
The Little Book of Icelandic,
by Alda Sigmundsdóttir.
For more information please visit
aldasigmunds.com/books

Hatching new words

So how does the Icelandic Language Committee come up with new words, or "neologisms" as they are called?

Recycling old words The Icelanders are terrible at recycling stuff, but they're actually pretty good at recycling words. Here the lingo committee reaches deep into Icelandic history to discover words that are no longer actively used, but which once upon a time had meaning. Probably the best known is *sími* (telephone) which originally meant "long thread". When the Icelanders were stuck for a name for "telephone" they thought of the wire needed to transport the voice and remembered that way back in yonder days there had been this word. So sími became the word for phone. Today, of course, we no longer have long threads that allow you to

talk to your grandmother or auntie - we use cellular networks for that. So naturally the language committee had invent a word for cellphone or mobile phone and they didn't deliberate long - *farsími* was the word of the day, made up of the prefix *far-* (migratory) and sími - "migratory phone".

THE LITTLE BOOK OF TOURISTS IN ICELAND

Third edition, 2023

Little Books Publishing
Reykjavík, 2017

Layout and cover design: Erlingur Páll Ingvarsson
Illustrations: Megan Herbert

ISBN: 978-1-970125-17-7

LITTLE BOOKS
PUBLISHING

Made in United States
North Haven, CT
04 August 2023